GARLAND STUDIES IN

ENTREPRENEURSHIP

edited by
STUART BRUCHEY
ALLAN NEVINS PROFESSOR EMERITUS
COLUMBIA UNIVERSITY

A GARLAND SERIES

KOREAN IMMIGRANT ENTREPRENEURS

NETWORK AND ETHNIC RESOURCES

JIN-KYUNG YOO

GARLAND PUBLISHING, INC.
A MEMBER OF THE TAYLOR & FRANCIS GROUP
NEW YORK & LONDON / 1998

Library of Congress Cataloging-in-Publication Data

Yoo, Jin-Kyung, 1961–
    Korean immigrant entrepreneurs : network and ethnic
resources / Jin-Kyung Yoo.
        p.   cm. — (Garland studies in entrepreneurship)
    Includes bibliographical references and index.
    ISBN 0-8153-3203-3 (alk. paper)
    1. Korean American business enterprises. 2. Korean Ameri-
can businesspeople—Interviews. 3. Business networks—United
States. 4. Entrepreneurship—United States. I. Title. II. Series.
HD2344.5.U6Y66
338.6'422'089957073—dc21
                                                              98-37494

Printed on acid-free, 250-year-life paper
Manufactured in the United States of America

To my Mother

Contents

Tables and Figures

Acknowledgments

Most of all, I want to thank the Department of Sociology at the University of Georgia that provided all the resources for this research to emerge. Without the support of the department for many years, this study would not have been possible. In addition, my thanks goes to my major professor, Dr. William Finlay, and all the committee members for my dissertation, Dr. Barry Schwartz, Dr. Woody Beck, Dr. Linda Grant, and Dr. James Coverdill for their suggestions and time to put forward for this research.

My sincere acknowledgment goes to Dr. Leann Tigges, University of Wisconsin, who helped place the corner stone for this project. At the very early stage of this project, she spent much time with me, discussing the issues and ideas. On the basis of these conversations, I have been able to design, pursue, and develop this research further.

I deeply appreciate Dr. Ivan Light, University of California, Los Angeles, for providing valuable insights and suggestions. His comments enhanced the strength of my arguments in this study.

My sincere thanks also goes to all the 159 Korean entrepreneurs in the Atlanta Metropolitan area who have been interviewed. They have provided rich information for this study of immigrant entrepreneurship in the United States. They were willing to spend long hours for interviews during their busy business operation hours. They are the fundamental contributors for this research. In addition, my thanks goes to Dr. Pyong-Gap Min , the Queens College of Cuny, and Dr. In-Jin Yoon, Korea University. They facilitated me with helpful advise and information as I began this project for my Ph.D. dissertation.

I appreciate my parents, sisters and brothers for always being there ready to give me both mental and material support all through the years of my graduate school and further. If it was not for their devoted support that helped me sustain the hardship in my life, neither this book nor my Ph.D. degree would have been possible.

My thanks also goes to my husband and an Astronomer, Thomas Hearty, for his time and support through the entire process of writing this book. He is the best companion for my scholarly life.

Korean Immigrant Entrepreneurs

CHAPTER I

Introduction

Immigrants in the United States take distinctive paths towards economic assimilation because they have different experiences in the labor market from those of both the majority and other native-born minorities. Immigrants are compelled to have marginal occupations due partially to their lack of resources (e.g., labor market information), and partially to their insufficient language skills or untransferable mechanical skills. With these handicaps in the mainstream labor market, immigrants tend to pursue alternative occupations to overcome their marginal occupational positions. The alternative occupation is often found in entrepreneurship and creates a tendency toward over-representation of immigrants in entrepreneurship (Light and Sanchez, 1987; Light, 1980; Portes and Manning, 1986; Wilson and Portes, 1980).

It has been a historical trend that immigrants in the United States pursue entrepreneurship to achieve economic affluence, as did Jews, Greeks, and Italians from the late 19th century (Glazer and Moynihan, 1963), and Chinese and Japanese at the turn of the century (Light, 1972). However, it has been found that only certain immigrant groups are likely to establish small businesses and move up in the socio-economic hierarchy (Hoffman and Marger, 1991). Among them, Koreans are an immigrant group with one of the highest proportions of self-employed entrepreneurs (Bonacich et al., 1977; Bonacich and Jung, 1982; Light, 1980; Light and Bonacich, 1988; Min, 1988; I. Kim, 1987; Kim and Hurh, 1985; Portes and Manning, 1986; Waldinger, 1989; Waldinger and Aldrich, 1990). Fratoe (1986) found that Korean immigrants have the highest proportion of self-employed entrepreneurs among Asian immigrants and one of the highest among all immigrants in the United States. Previous studies indicate that more than one-third of Korean heads of household in Los Angeles, New York, and Atlanta are engaged in small businesses (I.Kim, 1981; Min, 1988, 1996; Yu, 1982).

There are various arguments over the causes for immigrants' concentration in entrepreneurship as well as over the factors which cause entrepreneurship to become a passageway to economic mobility and achievement for immigrants. However, there are no thorough answers for how immigrants become capable of instigating a hospitable entrepreneurial environment due to partial consideration or misinterpretation of the factors. For instance, networks and class resources as determined by educational background have never been examined simultaneously and networks are sometimes misinterpreted as ethnic resources.

Previous investigations have shown that educational background is a crucial factor for ethnic entrepreneurship (Bates, 1994a; 1994b; 1997). However, these investigations do not provide evidence for why educational background is important or how it is capitalized for small businesses. In addition, other studies have found the tremendous importance of networks utilized for ethnic entrepreneurship (Aldrich and Zimmer, 1986). However, since they do not contemplate networks in conjunction with educational background, they cannot explain how different networks generate different resources. Likewise, most network researchers contemplate networks without distinguishing social networks and family networks despite their distinctive characteristics and operation. Furthermore, some studies consider social networks and family networks as kinds of ethnic resources along with unpaid family labor or rotating credit associations (RCA). As a result, there is a significant shortcoming in understanding of what kinds of resources are generated on the basis of these different networks.

Therefore, it is important to examine the interactions and reciprocal influences of networks, educational background, and ethnic resources systemically to have a comprehensive understanding of these factors. We can have better understanding of ethnic entrepreneurship (i.e., the incentives that compel or encourage immigrants to enter entrepreneurship, and the factors that capacitate immigrants to achieve entrepreneurship), only when we contemplate these factors simultaneously.

One of the most vital aspects for immigrant entrepreneurship is resource mobilization. Korean immigrant entrepreneurs, like all entrepreneurs, enthusiastically collect necessary resources to establish businesses, the resources such as what kinds of businesses they will run, which kinds of businesses have a stable economic performance, which kinds of businesses demand less physical labor or have reasonable hours to work, how much financial capital different kinds of businesses require, how they are going to provide business capital, whether they are going to borrow financial captial in addition to their personal savings, if they borrow, whom they are going to borrow from, and most of all, whom they are going to contact to gain all this information.

Thus, to address all these issues, this study will focus on five major issues: (1) the relationships between networks and class resources as determined by educational background; (2) the distinctions between social networks and family networks; (3) the utilization of social networks and family networks for business establishment by Korean immigrants; (4) the factors that split Korean entrepreneurs into two economic niches, inside the enclave and outside it; (5) the utilization of ethnic resources for Korean business entrepreneurship.

The high representation of Korean immigrants in small entrepreneurship started with the Korean immigrant groups who came after the Immigration and Nationality Act Amendments of 1965. The 1965 Amendments emphasize immigrants' credential background and eliminate national preferences. As a result, the demographics of Korean immigrants since 1965 have changed to an urbanized, white collar, highly educated segment of the Korean population (Light, 1980; I.Kim, 1981, 1987; Kim and Hurh, 1985; Min, 1988; Waldinger, 1989), and the number of Korean immigrants has also drastically increased (Immigration and Naturalization Service, 1966-1993). Unlike most European immigrants at the turn of the century, who were peasants, had low educational backgrounds, and were from low strata of the countries of origin, the Korean immigrants from the late 1960s and the early 1970s had medical and managerial credentials and thus tried to blend into the "melting pot" with higher expectations regarding economic opportunities based on their educational and credential background. Despite their high occupational credentials, the jobs available for a vast majority of Korean immigrants have been low-wage and low-skilled occupations with a lack of job security or prospects (see Table 5-2 in Chapter V).

Researchers propose various theories to explain why Koreans, or most immigrants for that matter, tend to pursue and prefer entrepreneurship to employment in the mainstream labor market. Light (1979, 1980) develops a "reactive cultural theory" that immigrants tend to pursue entrepreneurship due to the hostility and disadvantages that they encounter in the labor market. As a reaction to disadvantages in the labor market, a group develops solidarity in the ethnic community. In addition, immigrants tend to have unique cultural resources and some immigrated with class resources brought with them from the country of origin.

Light, therefore, argues that a disadvantaged group creates an entrepreneurial environment as a reaction to a disadvantageous situation by using such resources. As an example of ethnic resources, Light (1972) and Light et al. (1990) present "rotating credit associations" (RCA) which they found a large number of Asian immigrants, including Korean immigrants, utilize as a capital resource. In addition, a frugal attitude and a strong ethic for a hard working attitude among Korean immigrants are counted as crucial factors to establish an entrepreneurial environment.

However, this theory cannot fully explain differences in participation rates in entrepreneurship among ethnic groups and minorities, because the theory lacks explanations for the fact that not all disadvantaged minorities develop an entrepreneurial environment. That is, it overlooks the disadvantageous situation and attitudes of certain immigrant groups that cannot create an environment for ethnic entrepreneurship.

A structuralist approach, proposed by Bonacich (1973), argues for a "split labor market," providing opportunities for immigrants to become a "middleman minority" which mediates by connecting producer and consumer, owner and renter, the elite and the masses. In the economic structure, there is a gap between large and monopolized economies and small and marginal economies. Although the large economy is served by large companies, the small economy is left under- or unserved by the large economy. The small economy is mostly located in the neighborhoods where people in low strata of society are concentrated, such as inner city neighbors. The underserved economy therefore provides an opportunity for immigrants to enter as a middleman minority, who connects the large and small economies and delivers services to the underserved economy.

In addition, structuralists argue that the generally small size of immigrant entrepreneurship gives a resilience and advantage in industries where demands fluctuate and fashions continue to change

(Morokvasic et al., 1990). Large firms do not go into an industry that has continuously changing fashions or demands, which prevent mass production on assembly lines. Therefore, industries such as the garment industry are more suitable for immigrant entrepreneurs with small capital, because they do not need to compete with large companies. Moreover, considering that those industries are labor intensive, immigrant entrepreneurs are in an advantageous situation, because they can produce goods at a cheap price by pulling cheap labor from coethnic laborers and their small size enables them to adjust to fluctuating demand (Bailey and Waldinger, 1991).

However, structural theory also overlooks the fact that not all immigrant groups or minorities manage to utilize those structural opportunities in the economy. Since entrepreneurship requires a variety of resources to start, the theory also overlooks that initial conditions make only certain groups, such as Korean immigrants, likely or able to go into entrepreneurship.

On the other hand, another of structural theory, rooted in the notion of the enclave economy, argues that immigrants are prone to be entrepreneurs because of the following crucial elements, which favor immigrant entrepreneurship: (1) a large body of immigrants with entrepreneurial backgrounds; (2) availability of capital and a source of cheap labor from coethnic members; and (3) a captive market where immigrant entrepreneurs offer services with cultural goods to the coethnic customers (Portes and Manning, 1986; Wilson and Portes, 1980). However, the theory does not explain why or how immigrant entrepreneurs manage to cater to non-coethnic clientele. Considering that Korean entrepreneurs who cater outside the enclave economy are more numerous and prosperous than those inside the enclave, this omission is a serious oversight. However, the enclave theory provides an important criterion to investigate immigrant entrepreneurship in the enclave economy and non-enclave economy. Since Korean immigrant businesses show significant differences between the ways in which they mobilize resources in the enclave economy and outside it, it is important to examine the enclave businesses separately from the non-enclave businesses.

Min (1983) suggests a more personal factor, "status inconsistency," as a reason why Korean immigrants turn to entrepreneurship. He found that there is a sharp contrast between the jobs that Korean immigrants held in Korea and those they held in the United States. The vast majority of Korean immigrants tend to find their first occupation near the bottom of the occupational hierarchy, whereas over 90% of the respondents in his study have had professional or white-collar office jobs in Korea. As a result, Korean immigrants tend to be underemployed despite their educational backgrounds, which creates frustration. Min (1983), thus, argues that frustration encourages them to pursue an alternative occupation in entrepreneurship.

Regarding the existing theories, it seems that most lack an explanation of the movement of immigrants or ethnic minorities away from employment in the mainstream labor market. Most of all, most theories do not present a thorough explanation of what enables them to establish an entrepreneurial environment. Since the entire process involving immigrant entrepreneurship is closely related to the kinds of resources that an ethnic group possesses and how well they generate them, ethnic entrepreneurship should be investigated by considering what the foundations of resource mobilization to establish an entrepreneurial environment are.

There are various ways to mobilize resources. Network theorists argue that social ties are the foremost source that facilitates immigrants with information, resources, and social support (Zimmer and Aldrich, 1986). In fact, research has found that network ties not only help them to immigrate to a new land (Massey, 1988), but also provide fundamental resources to get into entrepreneurship to begin with (Werbner, 1990). As a result, networks become indispensable for entrepreneurship from founding to success, because they furnish capital and labor supplies and update business information (Zimmer and Aldrich, 1987; Werbner, 1987).

However, although network theories examine how immigrants utilize networks for adjustment in a new society and for economic pursuits, networks have not been extensively examined in terms of the differences in the characteristics among the variety of networks and the establishment of networks in the ethnic community after immigration. When immigrants come to a destination, regardless of their possession of family networks already established before immigration, they tend to exuberantly participate in a process of network establishment in the community. Although previous studies provide explanations for the utilization of networks for immigrant entrepreneurship, they tend to focus only on how existing networks in communities operate for entrepreneurship, disregarding the global context of networks, such as the process of network establishment, the ways network operate among the members of the business community, and most of all, how different networks generate different resources on the basis of their characteristics. As a result, previous network studies have resulted in a fragmentary picture of network establishment and utilization.

However, networks have various forms and characteristics and are established in a variety of ways. Among networks, the most vivid types are family networks and social networks. Family networks are established by chain migrants who came with the legal help of their family members in the United States. On the other hand, immigrants tend to follow typical patterns in establishing social networks. For instance, Pakistanis in Britain tend to establish social networks at the destination on the basis of geographic origin and cast status in Pakistan before immigration (Werbner, 1984), and Korean immigrants in America tend to establish networks on the basis of educational background in Korea (Yoo, 1996). If networks are such fundamental sources for resource mobilization, differences in the types of networks may influence the kinds of resources generated from the networks. In addition, there are misconceptions and shortcomings in the understanding in immigrant networks, in that some studies perceive networks as ethnic resources, some examine only one aspect of either social or family networks, and others consider both family and social networks as one concept.

However, since immigrants establish networks with specific intentions to facilitate business establishment and operation, network establishment should be considered as an economic activity rather than an ethnic solidarity. Furthermore, social and family networks are distinctive networks that are established and operated for different purposes. Therefore, this study focuses closely on how networks are established to serve as sources of resource mobilization, how the established networks facilitate Korean immigrants to start entrepreneurship, and how different networks operated distinctly to generate different resources for entrepreneurship. Therefore, this study separates family networks from social networks to see differences in the resources generated by networks on the basis of the differences in their characteristics. Further, this study examines how resources influence Koran immigrants to enter different economic niches, either the enclave or non-enclave.

Many studies on immigrant entrepreneurship rely solely on Census data (Bates, 1994a, 1994b, 1997). However, these studies can lead to a significant misunderstanding in ethnic or immigrant entrepreneurship since they do not acknowledge the significance of social resources such as networks and ethnic resources. Although these studies show that those with high educational background and high financial capital are successful in small business, they do not explain what role educational background plays.

Although it is true that ethnic entrepreneurs with relatively large firms tend to rely less on social resources (Bates, 1997), studies that rely solely on Census data overlook that the entrepreneurs with larger businesses have previously relied on social resources to develop their small businesses to lager ones by repeatedly selling their small business and buying larger ones. In addition, ethnic entrepreneurs, who attain large businesses and do not need social resources as fundamentally as when they had small businesses, become a source for other small business owners and ethnic members who pursue entrepreneurship. Moreover, this analysis finds that the entrepreneurs who collected information through social networks tend to start businesses with higher economic returns. Bates (1997) tested whether the presence of unpaid family labor is a factor that influences immigrants to enter entrepreneurship. However, the assumption itself is impractical according to data collected through face-to-face interviews for this study. It will be shown in Chapter VII that unpaid family labor is a favorable factor for ethnic businesses only after businesses are established and there is no use for unpaid family labor when immigrants begin the pursuit of entrepreneurship.

Therefore, although Census data contributes information about general characteristics of immigrant entrepreneurs and cover a large number of business owners and a wide range of geographic locations in the United States, these researches lack information on individual characteristics and resources that were brought from the country of origin or that have been acquired after immigration. The individual characteristics include social and ethnic resources in the community that are helpful for developing an entrepreneurial environment in a new country (i.e., the ways in which immigrants mobilize resources necessary for business establishment, the kinds of resources available for them to utilize, or the kinds of prior employment experiences after immigration which might have helped them establish businesses). Since these individual characteristics have fundamental importance for immigrant entrepreneurship, data collected in Atlanta through face-to-face interviews furnishes much more detailed and rich information, such as sources and methods of resource mobilization, their prior employment experiences of entrepreneurs, the ethnicity of their employers, and the benefits of their prior employment experiences to their business establishments.

There are many studies of Korean entrepreneurship in Los Angeles, New York, or Chicago, where the history of Korean communities is lengthy ranging from three decades to over a century old, and where the size of the Korean communities is much larger than that in Atlanta (I.Kim, 1981; Waldinger, 1989; Kim and Hurh, 1985; Yoon, 1991c). Although Korean immigration to Atlanta began approximately from the mid-1970s (Min, 1983), the Korean community in Atlanta did not become as noticeably large as it is today until the late 1980s (The Southeast Newspaper Weekly, 1996). Although there is an earlier study of the Atlanta Korean community (Min, 1983), the community was much smaller, with about 280 Korean business establishments and not anywhere near the current size of over 1,000 business establishments. Thus, the ethnic economy in the Korean community had yet to be established even by the early 1980s, and most Korean businesses were located outside the enclave close to inner city neighborhoods (Min, 1983). As a result of its short history and ongoing growth, the Korean community in Atlanta displays the dynamics of resource mobilization and network establishments that one cannot find in Korean immigrant communities with longer histories. Therefore, this study about Korean entrepreneurship in Atlanta in the mid-1990s provide unique context of information, because the history of the Korean community is still short.

Chapter II reviews the literature related to immigrant or minority entrepreneurship, contemplating network theory, cultural theory, and structural theory. The network theory posits how potential immigrants become motivated to be mobile by attaining information about economic and social conditions of the host society through network ties in a foreign country. In addition, the theory describes the entrepreneurial pursuit of immigrants after immigration, explaining utilization of networks and obtainment of social and economic mobility through networks.

On the other hand, cultural theory argues that the values and orientations of entrepreneurship are embedded in some ethnic groups and examines the ethnic resources and class resources that are utilized for business establishment and operation. The theory argues that disadvantaged ethnic or immigrant groups with ethnic and class resources are in a rather favorable situation to engage in entrepreneurship, in that they can convert the disadvantageous situations into incentives for becoming entrepreneurs by utilizing ethnic and class resources. In addition, there are opportunity structures which allow immigrants to enter entrepreneurship (e.g., the enclave economy, the underserved economy, or the small size economy). The theory argues that these unique economic structures are favorable for immigrants to establish businesses by utilizing their distinctive resources such as their strategy of self-exploitation through long working hours, the insulation of the coethnic market, and ethnic resources.

Therefore, this study attempts to reconcile these theories by investigating all of the factors simultaneously, since immigrant entrepreneurship is created as a result of a combination of various factors and environments including different social and individual elements such as ethnic (e.g., frugal attitude, unpaid family labor, and rotating credit association), structural (e.g., advantageous and/or disadvantageous structural opportunities for immigrants), and individual factors (e.g., class resources and networks).

Chapter III discusses data and methods. To comprehend Korean businesses better and in depth, the analyses employ two methods: descriptive statistics and narrative analysis. The descriptive statistics are used to analyze the general tendencies of the economic pursuits and entrepreneurial activities of Korean immigrants. The narrative analysis explores textual issues such as prior employment experiences, ethnicity of prior employers, sources of resource mobilization for business establishment and maintenance, and the impact of deficient language skills, limited opportunities in the labor market, and discriminations.

The data is collected through face-to-face interviews with 159 Korean entrepreneurs who owned businesses in the Atlanta Metropolitan Area from April to November of 1994. The interviews were conducted in Korean based on a structured questionnaire (see Appendix). The sample is selected via three schemes for businesses in the enclave and non-enclave economies. Businesses in the enclave are selected randomly from a list developed based on advertisements in three Korean community newspapers. Only businesses which advertised three consecutive times are selected, since active advertisement indicates that businesses are currently actively operated.

Most businesses outside the enclave economy are selected randomly, based on lists provided by business associations, and the rest are selected by block sampling for businesses without associations. The lists of businesses catering to non-Korean customers was obtained from the presidents of the business associations. The most numerous businesses such as groceries, liquor stores, and dry cleaning/coin laundry stores have business associations, which provide lists of businesses of these kinds in Atlanta. Since the businesses tend to be geographically scattered, and located near residential areas, they are selected randomly from the lists. On the other hand, those without associations tend to be clustered in the Five Points area of downtown Atlanta or clustered on large streets, which enable block sampling. The blocks were selected on the basis of size of a cluster of Korean businesses catering non-Korean customers.

Chapter IV shows general tendencies and characteristics of Korean immigrants since the 1960s, demonstrating the number of Korean immigrants admitted over time, the changes in demographics (i.e., occupational backgrounds), and the mechanisms of admittance as immigrants to the United States. Although Korean immigration is a century old, massive immigration has started since the mid-1960s. Over time, the demographics of Korean immigrants have changed: laborers on the sugar plantation in Hawaii at the turn of the century; students and political refugees during the Japanese colonization until 1945; war orphans, wives of American serviceman in Korea, and students until the mid-1960s; those with credential backgrounds of professionals or managers until the mid-1970s; chain-migrants in the 1980s. These changes have been influenced by political, social, and economic conditions in Korea. Most of all, they were influenced by the implementation of various immigration laws in the United States.

Chapter V discusses the background of Korean entrepreneurs in Atlanta on the basis of time of immigration, educational background, and possession of family networks. Also the chapter evaluates network and cultural theories in the context of Korean immigrants in Atlanta based on their educational levels and possession of family networks through chain-migration. The purpose of the analysis is to determine influences of family networks and class resources on employment opportunities in the enclave labor market and on readiness to start businesses. In addition, it examines factors that motivate Korean immigrants to pursue entrepreneurship and avoid employment opportunities in the mainstream labor market.

Family networks have been recognized as one of the most prominent resources for immigrants, which enhance economic prospects for employment or career opportunities, reduce the risks involved in long-distance migration, and most of all generate capital and information for entrepreneurial pursuits (Goldberg, 1985; Light et al., 1993; Sanders and Nee, 1996; White, 1970). Given the general notion of the economic advantages of family networks, Korean entrepreneurs in Atlanta are analyzed based on the possession of family networks to gain an assessment of the advantages of family networks. However, this study shows that family networks are not such a strong factor for establishing businesses in shorter periods, for getting into entrepreneurship without suffering in marginal occupations, or for getting jobs in Korean-owned businesses to learn skills for business operations. Instead, class resources as measured by educational level have a consistent impact on shortening the period taken for the establishment of the first businesses and on getting into entrepreneurship without employment experiences in marginal occupations. In addition, the timing of immigration has a strong influence on job opportunities in Korean businesses, in that a much higher proportion of later immigrants who came since the 1980s have employment experiences with Korean employers. Therefore, the argument of the current network theory that family networks are crucial for immigrants' economic pursuit and success is not supported by this investigation of the Korean entrepreneurs in Atlanta. However, it does not mean that network theory should be abandoned. But rather, analysis of networks should be changed, so that family networks are examined separately from social networks. This will enable future investigations to see how the two types of networks generate different resources on the basis of their characteristics, and how networks have reciprocal influence with educational background. These analysis will be in Chapter VI.

Chapter VI examines ways in which Korean immigrant entrepreneurs mobilize resources by integrating networks and class resources. The chapter analyzes networks and educational background by showing how education influences the kinds of networks that entrepreneurs establish and use them to mobilize information and capital. Since most network theories do not distinguish between family networks and social networks, considering either all networks in one concept of networks or only one of the two types of networks, network theories are not able to explain why family networks are not such an advantageous resource for Korean immigrants in Atlanta. Therefore, the analysis of networks separates social networks from family networks to find out how different networks are utilized to generate different resources.

Generally, Korean immigrants enthusiastically establish social networks after immigration, regardless of their possession of family networks, because social networks are another major source for generating resources other than family networks. Social networks are established through involvement in Korean church and community organizations or associations.

To get into entrepreneurship, the most fundamental resources necessary are capital and business information. To mobilize these resources, Korean entrepreneurs utilize either family networks possessed before immigration and/or social networks established after immigration. This study shows that Korean entrepreneurs make wide use of family networks for financial support, whereas they tend to depend on social networks to mobilize business information and acquire skills for business operation. Therefore, this analysis uncovers tendencies, which network theories have overlooked, that family networks and social networks contribute to mobilize different resources. Furthermore, this analysis shows the possibility that resources generated from different sources bring about different results in the pursuit of entrepreneurship. That is, a difference in the origin of resources induces a difference in the occupancy of economic niches. The effects of the resources are discussed further in Chapter VII.

The analysis in Chapter VII combines all three approaches— analysis of family networks, social networks, and ethnic resources—to explain the factors that determine which economic niches entrepreneurs enter. There are two entrepreneurial niches for Korean immigrants to occupy. One is an economic niche in the enclave economy where the majority of customer are Koreans, selling cultural goods. The other is outside the enclave economy, mostly located in inner city neighborhoods, and catering to black residents. A few other businesses outside the enclave economy cater to middle class neighbors.

Korean entrepreneurs prefer to operate businesses outside the enclave economy, due to the higher economic returns, which most interviewees indicated. Therefore, Chapter VII examines how resources influence the establishment of businesses in different economic niches, either in the enclave or in the non-enclave. The factors, that induce entrepreneurs to occupy different economic niches, include social networks, family networks, and ethnic resources (i.e., unpaid family labor, coethnic labor, and hard working or frugal altitudes).

This analysis shows that social networks are crucial to enter the economic niches with higher economic returns. That is, Korean entrepreneurs utilize social networks far more frequently for business information in order to start businesses in the non-enclave economy. This tendency indicates that information acquired through social networks is valuable for Korean entrepreneurs who want to go into the non-enclave economy where businesses promise higher economic returns. In addition, although Korean immigrant entrepreneurs utilize family networks more often for financial capital, family networks do not seem to influence which economic niches Korean immigrants occupy.

In addition, although ethnic resources such as unpaid family labor, cheap coethnic labor, RCA, and a frugal attitude are often regarded as advantages for ethnic business establishment, these ethnic resources are important resources only after a business is operating, rather than for its establishment. Therefore, ethnic resources give Korean immigrant entrepreneurs a competitive advantage that native minorities lack. On the other hand, these ethnic resources do not give such an advantage in the early stages of business establishment or lead Korean entrepreneurs to occupy economic niches with better economic returns. In addition, an ethnic resource such as cheap coethnic labor is no longer available in the community, because Korean coethnic labor is now more expensive than other ethnic labor.

CHAPTER II

Literature Review

Immigrant entrepreneurship is created as a result of a consolidation of various factors and elements such as ethnic factors (e.g., frugal attitude, unpaid family labor, and rotating credit association), structural factors (e.g., advantageous and/or disadvantageous structural opportunities for immigrants), and individual factors (e.g., class resources and networks). Therefore, ethnic entrepreneurship should be explained by investigating all these factors simultaneously.

The theories to be discussed to understand the factors influencing immigrant entrepreneurship are: (1) network theory, which describes the steps of the immigration and assimilation processes, and which also delineates resource mobilization necessary for business establishment and management; (2) cultural theory, which explains immigrants' cultural domains brought from the country of origin and utilized as ethnic resources for immigrant entrepreneurship. The theory also describes how immigrants utilize the resources for economic assimilation to the host society; (3) and structural theory, which posits structural advantages and/or disadvantages, that immigrants fit efficiently into the economic structures, and that immigrants are encouraged to enter into entrepreneurship despite the risks of failure and high competition.

NETWORK THEORIES

Network theories enable a better understanding of two major immigration processes: the decision-making process of migration, and labor market incorporation and social mobility in the host society (Aldrich and Zimmer, 1986; De Jong and Gardner, 1981; Goldberg;

1985; Griego, 1987; Werbner, 1984, 1987, 1990). The first assumption explains how potential immigrants would or might be motivated to be mobile by attaining information about economic and social conditions of the host society through network ties in a foreign country. The motivation for immigration comes from the belief that the cost and risk can be reduced by acquiring information from network ties. The second concept entails the process of economic assimilation of immigrants' to a new society, the process in which migrants utilize social resources that are mobilized from networks and that help immigrants obtain social and economic mobility. In these two concepts, network theories attempt to explain how one decides to stay or to immigrate, and how one gets economic and/or psychological support for assimilation into the host society.

Network Establishment

Dependency theory explains international migration by focusing on the macro structure in the economies of both sending and receiving countries. The economic dependency theory conceptualizes that the economic dependency of less developed counties on more developed countries frames pull-and-push factors (Sassen-Koob, 1980; Piore, 1979; Portes, 1978, 1987). The theory argues that the "world capitalist system" which penetrates the economic systems in Third World societies results in peasants of the Third World societies becoming a source of cheap labor (Bonacich and Cheng, 1984: 1-56; Portes, 1978). Demand for cheap labor in the industrialized countries ultimately attracts those peasants to immigrate and they become a "reserve army of labor" in the more industrialized countries. Therefore, the theory perceives international migraion on the basis of the pull-and-push framework of migration that is bounded by economic motivations.

However, network theorists argue that economic dependency theory leaves the micro- or middle-range social structure unexplained for international immigration. Therefore, network theory rejects focusing exclusively on economic structures to explain international migration, but rather focuses on how social networks influence potential migrants to become motivated to immigrate by analyzing rather small units such as communities or households, instead of addressing entire economic structures. Therefore, the theory examines how networks are established, structured, and facilitated by immigrants for international migration (Massey, 1988; Morawska, 1989; Tilly, 1990; Taylor, 1986).

Networks include any type of interpersonally connected social ties that influence migrants in the entire migration process, before and after the migration. A network can constrain or facilitate the action of people, and thereby goes beyond simple individual links and becomes a social structure (Aldrich and Zimmer, 1986). Massey et al. (1987) note the development of networks in the process of immigration as follows:

> These ties bind migrants and non-migrants within a complex web of complementary social roles and interpersonal relationships that are maintained by an informal set of mutual expectations and prescribed behaviors. The social relationships that constitute migrant networks are not unique to migrants but develop as a result of universal human bonds that are molded to the special circumstances of international migration. These social ties are not created by the migratory process but are adapted to it and over time are reinforced by the common experience of migration itself (p.140-141).

Networks are positive determinants in individual decision making during immigration (Todaro, 1980). Information available at the destination is a vital element for the decision on whether or not to migrate, in that it provides a decision maker with better approaches and helps one to increase the expected return or spread the risk. Taylor (1986) illuminates one of the significant roles played by networks as follows:

> A particularly important role that migration networks seem to play in household labor decisions is in regard to risk. The household, when it makes its labor allocation plan, does not know with certainty what its rewards from investing in migration and other economic activities will be. The level and variability of the returns to migration (that is, migrant remittances) can be influenced to the extent the migrant has a support structure at the destination that enables him to respond effectively to the uncertainties around him. Migration networks can provide the migrant with information vital to his success in reaching his destination and in finding and retaining advantageous employment once he is there (p. 148-149).

As Taylor argues, network ties are one of the most crucial constituents for securing migrants' occupations and their adjustment in the new society, especially for international immigrants. The most decisive factor that influences the dynamics of the movement of individuals or groups from one place to another is the economic prospects of employment or career opportunities in the destination acquired through networks (White, 1970). Network theorists argue that ties emerge through the structural interdependency of both sending and receiving countries (Massey et al., 1987; Massey, 1988).

Historically, migrant flow has almost always been from economically less developed countries to more developed countries (Hugo, 1981; Massey, 1988; Morawska, 1989; Portes, 1978; Tilly, 1990). When countries are interrelated by economic exchanges, transportation and communication tend to develop along with the economic connections between the two countries. Such connections bring information about the job markets and economic conditions in the destination countries.

Accordingly, favorable information about more developed countries will encourage people in the less developed countries to migrate: for example, the economic relationship between European countries and the United States in the 19th century as well as at the beginning of the 20th century (Morawska, 1989; Tilly, 1990) brought massive numbers of immigrants from Europe; the relationship between Mexico and the United States in the late 20th century has been similar (Massey et al., 1987; Massey, 1988). Information, as a resource, not only encourages, but empowers people in the less developed countries to migrate for better economic opportunities. Therefore, the structural interconnection between the sending country and the receiving country functions as an essential component of migration network establishment as well as a motivation for immigration.

Migration networks expand over time and draw more people to utilize the networks for migration, because the migration networks have an "accumulative causation" (Massey, 1988; Morawska, 1989). Some courageous people immigrate using known channels established through connected social structures between two societies. These few people ultimately become a cornerstone of the network connections between the two societies. Though the effect might be trivial at first, the established networks assist potential immigrants to become mobile and eventually expands the networks. As a result, although some immigrants might have come alone, migration is a social process and a collective movement that extends beyond the individual level (Tilly, 1990; Morawska, 1989).

Networks for Ethnic Entrepreneurship

In addition to the concept that networks motivate immigration, networks are closely related to the economic pursuits of immigrants in their job searches and economic mobilities. Numerous studies note that networks are one of the most crucial aspects in entrepreneurship (Aldrich and Zimmer, 1986; Zimmer and Aldrich, 1987; Brüderl and Preisendörfer, 1997; Goldberg, 1985; Werbner, 1990, 1987). Aldrich and Zimmer (1986) argue that the focus of economic activity should be contemplated as being "embedded in a social context, channeled and facilitated or constrained and inhibited by people's positions in social networks" (p.4).

In addition, Portes (1995) suggests a concept of social capital for entrepreneurship, that is "the capacity of individuals to command scarce resources by virtue of their membership in networks or broader social structures" (p.12). That is, through these connections, an ethnic group generates material resources or mental support for ethnic entrepreneurship such as business information, price discounts, or interest-free loans. Therefore, ethnic entrepreneurs develop personal connections and institutional organizations that yield network ties in the community and that, in turn, provide information or advice for business operations. Ethnic organizations not only create emotional bonds, but also organize themselves to represent the interests of their members in the main society.

Immigrant organizations tend to be founded on the basis of common bonds from the old countries. For example, Pakistani immigrants in England are organized on the basis of their social class background and regional origin in the old country (Werbner, 1990). Korean immigrants also organize such institutions as Protestant churches, business associations, and university alumni associations (I. Kim, 1981). In addition to their ostensible purposes, these organizations represent the political and economic interests of their members toward the main society. Therefore, the degree to which ethnic groups organize themselves in their community largely determines the success of the group (Light, 1972; Glazer and Moynihan, 1963).

Furthermore, through "ecological succession," networks preserve and avail business opportunities for coethnic members and in turn influence extensions of ethnic entrepreneurship. The ecological succession of businesses through networks describes individual relations or institutional connections. Light and Bonacich (1988) observed ecological succession through networks of Korean liquor businesses in Los Angeles. They observed that Korean entrepreneurs are likely to rely on informal channels to learn about business sites from a friend or family member. Korean businesses to be sold never come to the open market, and are instead sold to other coethnic members through social relations.

Networks influence ethnic entrepreneurship to the extent that networks become indispensable for the founding, success, and expansion of businesses. The social circle of a coethnic community not only enables its members to learn about business opportunities, it also enables them to establish mutual trust which helps them generate credit, get support, or borrow money for business founding (Werbner, 1984; Zimmer and Aldrich, 1987). As a result, networks in the coethnic community ensure access to capital, a labor supply, and updated business information (Werbner, 1987). The relationships in the ethnic community reenforce and reaffirm the stability and extent of networks (Massey et al., 1987: chapter 6; Werbner, 1984).

However, although network theory proposes that immigrants utilize networks for adjustment in a new society and for economic pursuits, networks have not been extensively examined in terms of how differences in the characteristics among a variety of networks generate different resources. For instance, networks have two distinctive elements: social networks and family networks. Since the two types of networks are established on the basis of different sources and operated differently, it may well be possible that the two types of networks generate different resources necessary for ethnic entrepreneurship.

In addition, network theorists tend either to perceive both family networks based on kin ties and social networks based on relationship with community members in one concept (Zimmer and Aldrich, 1987), or to perceive only one type of network (Werbner, 1987), which results in an incomplete understanding of networks. Some researchers, on the other hand, tend to perceive family and/or social networks as a kind of ethnic resource, along with various other ethnic resources such as frugal attitude, work ethic, or rotating credit associations (Goldscheider and Kobrin, 1980). As a result, network theory tends to overlook the distinction between family and social networks and the characteristics of various networks that determine the kinds of resources to be generated and the kinds of people to get benefits.

Furthermore, although relationships between networks and class resources (e.g., educational background) are indispensable, no network studies examine its establishment of networks and function in conjunction with class resources. Rubinson and Browne (1994) note that education background contributes to economic growth when it is combined with an appropriate situation. Therefore, the effect of networks on ethnic entrepreneurship should be examined simultaneously with educational background. By doing so, we can find the precise effect of educational background rather than arguing the effect of educational background in vague term as Bates (1994a, 1994b, 1997).

CULTURAL THEORY

Orthodox Cultural Components

The cultural elements of an ethnic group have been consistently considered as key sources of understanding ethnic entrepreneurship. These cultural elements have been considered as ethnic resources. The most orthodox cultural component is embedded entrepreneurial values. The theory argues that values and orientations of entrepreneurship are embedded in some ethnic groups such as Jews and Gypsies through the process of socialization (Chinoy, 1952; Jenkins, 1984; Light, 1972, 1984, 1985; Tsukashima, 1991). The values include such components as entrepreneurial ambition, motivation, and skills.

Orthodox cultural theory argues that, if an ethnic group has a propensity for being entrepreneurs, it is purely a matter of culture. Therefore, it is thought to be a predisposition for entrepreneurial values and ambitions that causes some particular groups to become more representative in entrepreneurship than others. Thus, Mars and Wards (1984) caution against underestimating values that an ethnic group might possess and argue for consideration of the idea that embedded values are the factors which determine the inter-ethnic differences in rates of engaging in businesses, because possession of entrepreneurial values will put certain group in a different position than those without.

However, orthodox cultural theory has been further divided into "class" resources and "ethnic" resources. Light and Bonacich draw a line between class resources and ethnic resources as follows:

Primary socialization is only the first stage and is later supported by institutions and life styles that control adult conduct. Nonetheless, primary socialization is an indispensable prerequisite of any cultural theory; all who share an entrepreneurial culture do so because they earlier learned the values, attitudes, motives, information, and skills of this culture in the course of socialization. . . . A class interpretation of entrepreneurship is also possible. Insofar as a bourgeoisie introduces its youth into business, entrepreneurship is the cultural aspect of inter-generational transmission. . . . [that] the bourgeoisie. . . . turns over to its children the entrepreneurial values, motivations, and skills requisite to reproducing the private economy. This is a cultural transmission. . . . The boundary between class and ethnic culture depends upon how generally entrepreneurial values, motivations, and skills are distributed among a population. Ethnic cultures are entrepreneurial when they distribute entrepreneurial motivation and skills among all socioeconomic levels. . . . class culture of entrepreneurship limits entrepreneurial values, motivations, and skills to the bourgeoisie. (279-281)

Ethnic resources contain ethnic institutions, sojourning orientation, relative satisfaction, and reactive solidarity, on the one hand; class resources include human capital, the means of production, and money to invest, on the other (Light, 1984, 1985). Ethnic resources are available for entire ethnic members to make use of; thereby ethnic resources are seen as socio-cultural features of the whole group which coethnic entrepreneurs utilize in business or from which their businesses benefit (Light and Bonacich, 1988: 178). On the other hand, class resources are available to a limited number of members in the community on the basis of possession of the means of production and human capital such as educational background.

Ethnic resources include tendencies that immigrants are satisfied with entrepreneurship which requires hard work because the rewards of working hard in entrepreneurship are relatively satisfying in comparison to the rewards attainable in their country of origin; immigrants create reactive solidarity and insulate their community in response to the hostile host society by excluding non-members; some immigrants have a tendency for return-migration, believing before immigration that their stay will be temporary.

The classic examples of ethnic entrepreneurship are Gypsy merchants, who profess to know how to tell fortunes, and who have historically been vividly represented in entrepreneurship. Jews have also had unmatched representation in entrepreneurship compared to other ethnic groups in America (Goldscheider and Kobrin, 1980). Goldscheider and Kobrin (1980) argue that this propensity is embedded in the culture of an ethnic group, because it is a learned attitude through socialization in that a father's involvement in self-employment had an extremely important effect for some groups for an inclination towards entrepreneurship. Scase and Goffee (1980) find more general evidence of cultural embeddedness in the general population, explaining that many people by nature reject working for someone else and are prone to become entrepreneurs.

In addition to the ethnic resource of an embedded entrepreneurial orientation, an important aspect of ethnic resources is whether a group retains practical ethnic resources that can be utilized in entrepreneurial activities. For instance, ethnic resources drawn from family savings and loans from coethnic members are also important for Korean entrepreneurs (Kim and Hurh, 1985). Another ethnic resource that has received much attention from researchers as a source of capital provision for ethnic entrepreneurs is the rotating credit associations (Geertz, 1962; Light, 1972; Light et al., 1990; I. Kim, 1981). By using the term "rotating credit association," coined by Geertz, Light and his colleague observed classic examples of the Chinese and Japanese at the turn of the century (Light, 1972) and Koreans in the late 20th century (Light et al., 1990). The association is considered as an outstanding example of ethnic resources that facilitate the social mobility of ethnic groups by providing capital for entrepreneurship.

Another ethnic resource available in the community is the various sources of labor (Light, 1984; Light and Bonacich, 1988; Portes and Manning, 1986; Werbner, 1984). Immigrants tend to find laborers within their ethnic communities, such as extended families and coethnic members, that are utilized as a valuable labor force for ethnic entrepreneurship (Waldinger, 1989). Researchers, such as Light and Bonacich (1988) in Los Angeles and Waldinger (1989) in New York, found an extensive usage of unpaid family labor as well as coethnic employees by Korean entrepreneurs. All such ethnic resources give a competitive advantage to ethnic entrepreneurs in businesses.

On the other hand, class resources have three elements: "previous experience in business; skills relevant to running a business; those less specific characteristics and qualities which will facilitate success in business" (Mars and Ward, 1984: 11). The class resources have two sides: psychological and material (Light, 1984, 1985). The psychological side is the same as the orthodox cultural argument, and contains entrepreneurial orientations inter-generationally handed down over time through socialization. The orientations consist of ambitions, motivations, attitudes, and institutions rather than financial assets (Light, 1980, 1985). The material side, on the other hand, refers to material possession or transfer over generations, of such material assets as the means of production, human capital, or entrepreneurial skills and knowledge. For instance, the difference in educational attainment is a useful indication of intraethnic differences in participation in self-employment (Kim et al., 1989). Therefore, cultural theorists argue that entrepreneurship requires not only material resources that are turned over to their children, but also entrepreneurial values, motivations, and skills (Light and Bonacich, 1988).

Reactive Cultural Theory

In contrast to a cultural theory based on ethnic or class resources, reactive cultural theory focuses on racial disadvantages rather than ethnic advantages, exclusion rather than exclusiveness (Aldrich et al., 1984). Light (1972, 1979, 1980) reconciles the cultural theory of ethnic advantages in entrepreneurship and the theory of racial disadvantages, and argues that "sometimes disadvantage occurs with entrepreneurial cultural endowment, and vice versa" (Light, 1979: 41).

Therefore, Light (1980) suggests a reconciled theory, a reactive interpretation of cultural entrepreneurship in disadvantaged situations. The theory posits circumstances in which immigrants encounter disadvantages, and yet have useful resources to become ethnic entrepreneurs, whereas native minorities lack such resources. The theory argues that disadvantaged ethnic groups with ethnic and class resources are in a rather favorable situation, because they can convert the disadvantageous situations into incentives for becoming entrepreneurs. Therefore, the reactive cultural theory suggests that ethnic entrepreneurship is to be understood as a situational response to disadvantaged and exclusionary circumstances against ethnic minorities such as immigrants in the United States (Bonacich, 1973; Waldinger, 1989), and that ethnic entrepreneurship is to be understood simultaneously in the context of unique cultural and ethnic elements that an ethnic group possesses (Light, 1972, 1979, 1980; Light and Bonacich, 1988).

Immigrants are naturally disadvantaged in the labor market due to barriers of language proficiency, unfamiliarity with the social system in the country of destination, and exclusion from the host society. They, therefore, are often excluded from attractive jobs in the labor market and constrained to make a living in marginal occupations (Bonacich, 1973; Aldrich et al., 1984). These immigrants, excluded from more desirable jobs, are drawn to entrepreneurship as a reaction to discriminatory opportunity structures in the labor market. Immigrants and minorities are not only driven from better economic opportunities in the general labor market, but also in the area of business, which results in them being found in the least desirable and marginal sectors of business (Mars and Wards, 1984). Given these disadvantages, reactive cultural theory argues that a crucial factor splitting minorities into those who turn to the business sphere and those who lag behind economically is whether or not the minorities possess cultural elements that later can generate useful resources for entrepreneurship.

Ethnic entrepreneurship has long been considered as an avenue for economic and social mobility for those immigrants who are disadvantaged in the labor market and who do not have inherited means of production. Nonetheless, small businesses are by nature marginal and vulnerable. However, although some ethnic groups might not have such values as inherited and learned entrepreneurial orientation through socialization, they become motivated for entrepreneurship to obtain economic mobility, if they have such resources as ethnic and class resources to utilize.

Forester (1978) perceives aspirations of Asian businesses as a result of the ambitious and optimistic attitude of the immigrants. For instance, Japanese and Chinese immigrants in the late 18th and early 19th centuries, who experienced discrimination, had concrete organizations which controlled ethnic businesses and information for co-members (Light, 1972). Researchers also conceive rotating credit associations run by Korean, Japanese, and Chinese immigrants as a primary source of capital, which is most crucial element for business investment and maintenance (Aldrich et al., 1984; Light 1972; Light et al., 1990). Kim and Hurh (1985) also found in Chicago that effective utilization of ethnic resources among Korean immigrants is crucial for their business establishments and operations, the ethnic resources that contribute to labor and financial capital through family, friends, and relatives. Given the existing disadvantageous situation, a group with beneficial resources can develop an entrepreneurial environment as an alternative to wage employment in the mainstream labor market. Hence, these resources are primary factors in determining the differing ratios in the representation of entrepreneurship among ethnic minorities.

STRUCTURAL THEORY

Structural Disadvantages

As briefly examined above, it is a pervasive notion that immigrants and minorities are disadvantaged in the labor market, since immigrants and minorities are systematically excluded from desirable employment opportunities (Piore, 1979; Doeringer and Piore, 1971; Bonacich 1972). With regard to ethnic entrepreneurship, those disadvantageous situations have been interpreted using the "middleman minority" thesis (Bonacich: 1973). Similarly to reactive cultural theory, middleman minority theory argues that immigrants pursue entrepreneurship due to limited employment opportunities in the labor market. However, this theory argues that they enter entrepreneurship because of a gap in the structure of the economy, rather than because of cultural advantages.

Therefore, Turner and Bonacich (1980) argue that cultural approaches tend to emphasize cultural traits, such as ethnic solidarity or rotating credit associations, in isolation without linking them to general patterns in the society. Therefore, Bonacich (1972, 1973) argues that ethnic antagonism should be scrutinized in tandem with analysis of the reasons why immigrants take the route of ethnic entrepreneurs as a "middleman minority." In other words, cultural traits cannot be judged without considering the social context that might foster as well as compel immigrants to become entrepreneurs. Thus, cultural traits should instead be examined in the social context in which immigrants operate.

The structuralists argue that disadvantages in the labor market are the most significant influences on immigrant entrepreneurship. For instance, there is a large wage differential for the same occupation in the labor market (Bonacich, 1972: 547). Bonacich argues that the wage difference among workers is not a result of race or ethnicity, but rather is due to differences in resources and motives, which often correlates with ethnicity. For example, immigrants are deficient in language and have incompatible work skills, which are vital components in the labor market. Deficiency and incompatibility, thus, cause lower labor prices.

Aldrich et al. (1984) also acknowledge structural disadvantages that precipitate an entrepreneurial environment among immigrants. They argue that immigrant entrepreneurship is more influenced by external forces than internal characteristics, the external forces that are in the opportunity structure within the receiving society. Discrimination by majorities' restrains minority's access to political power and social status (ibid: 193). As a consequence, immigrants suffer from un- or under-employment in a new land and are caught up in low-wage and low-skill jobs without the prospect of promotion.

Ultimately, these forms of powerlessness and frustration in the labor market and in the general society encourage immigrants to look for an alternative to undesirable employment or unemployment. The typical alternative is entrepreneurship as means of further economic achievement, such as Japanese penetration in California agriculture (Modell, 1977; Bonacich and Modell, 1980; Tsukashima, 1991) and Chinese laundromats and restaurant owners (Light, 1972).

However, disadvantaged minorities and immigrants cannot simply turn themselves into entrepreneurs, if a structural gap does not exist. As Bonacich (1973) argues, they become a "middleman minority" by taking advantage of the structural gap that is manifested by the dual structure of the labor market: the primary labor market is occupied by the majority; the secondary is occupied by ethnic groups who are driven away from being part of the larger society and who are there to be exploited.

Between the two structures, a structural gap is left without being served, and the middleman minority takes a role in it (Blalock, 1967; Bonacich, 1972, 1987). This gap is found by immigrants who fit themselves into it by establishing their own economic niches as a middleman minority. The role of the middleman minority is to mediate between elites and masses. The middleman minorities are used by American monopoly capitalism to deliver services to the least desired commercial places, such as inner city low-income neighborhoods, dealing directly with hostility, crime, and low profits (Blalock, 1967; Bonacich et al., 1976). By using middleman minorities, monopoly capitalism can avoid serving a market which has low profits and a harsh environment. Turner and Bonacich (1980) explain that the middleman minorities have the following social and economic traits:

> The prominent social characteristics of middleman minorities include: (a) the clear tendency to be migrants to a recipient society;

(b) the propensity to form and maintain a separate community or district in the recipient society; (c) the desire to maintain distinct cultural traits such as language, values, and religious beliefs; (d) the propensity to cultivate high degrees of internal solidarity through extended kinship ties, school and religious organizations, and preference for endogamy. . . . and probably most important in terms of distinguishing middleman minorities from other kinds of minorities, are distinctive economic traits: (a) the tendency to concentrate in a limited range of middle rank entrepreneurial economic roles, such as trading, small business, and independent professions. . . . (c) the ability to use pooled kin labor, to work extremely long hours, and to be thrifty; (d) and the maintenance of intragroup economic organizations, such as rotating credit associations and business leagues (p.146).

Therefore, for the disadvantage structuralists, the labor market disadvantages of ethnic minorities and the structural gap in the society coincide to bring about the emergence of an immigrant ethnic entrepreneurship (Bonacich, 1972).

Structural Advantages

Structural advantage theory, on the other hand, argues that there is an opportunity structure in the general economy (Morokrasic et al. 1990). The theory suggests that, to gain sight of the full picture of ethnic entrepreneurship, the opportunity structure should be considered along with the social structure of a particular immigrant group (Waldinger et al., 1985). That is, predisposing structural factors and strategies of resource mobilization of an ethnic group should be included for the comprehension of immigrant entrepreneurship.

Unlike the structural disadvantage argument, the advantage argument suggests that there are economic structures that immigrants can establish as their own economic niches, despite barriers and shortcomings in resources. Structural advantage theory argues that the immigrant ethnic economy should not be considered apart from the main economic structure, but rather as a part of it because the ethnic economy also consists of a context of the main economy, such as competition, as well as integration along the types of industries (Waldinger, 1986; Waldinger et al., 1990). Aldrich and Waldinger (1990) explain opportunity structures as follows:

The structure and allocation of opportunities open to potential ethnic business owners have been shaped by historically contingent circumstances. Groups can only work with the resources made available to them by their environments, and the structure of opportunities is constantly changing in modern industrial societies. Market conditions may favor only businesses serving an ethnic community's needs, in which case entrepreneurial opportunities are limited. Or, market conditions may favor smaller enterprises serving non- ethnic populations, in which case opportunities are much greater (p. 114).

The primary advantageous structure is in the enclave economy catering to the coethnic population (Portes and Manning, 1986). The theory of enclave economy has been developed to explain the structural advantages of the protected market in which ethnic entrepreneurs operate by providing primary services that neither the general market nor other ethnic groups can provide. The enclave economy has the characteristics that immigrants are spatially concentrated; less culturally assimilated; and often economically better off than native minorities (Wilson and Portes, 1980). The emergence of the enclave economy requires three latent components: first, the presence of a substantial number of immigrants with initial entrepreneurial experiences and skills; second, the availability of sources of capital; and third, the availability of sources of labor (Wilson and Portes, 1980; Portes and Manning, 1986). The enclave economy is established by immigrant entrepreneurs who make use of language, cultural traits, and ethnic tastes of the coethnic group.

The main characteristics of the enclave economy are paternalistic labor relations and strong community solidarity induced from reciprocal obligations attached to a common ethnicity (Wilson and Portes, 1980). The enclave economy functions in such a way that newcomers can get access to job opportunities and immigrant entrepreneurs have access to a source of cheap labor, characterizing a great degree of self-enclosed interdependence (Wilson and Martin, 1982). This interdependency generates an environment in which immigrant labor earns higher wages (Wilson and Portes, 1980) and newcomers have a better chance for skill acquisition (Bailey and Waldinger, 1991). Therefore, the protected enclave market gives competitive advantages to the coethnic entrepreneurs by identifying ethnicity and excluding non-members (Hannerz, 1974).

However, since enclave economy theory focuses exclusively on the protected market that is geographically clustered, it overlooks the existence of ethnic entrepreneurship located outside the enclave economy. For example, about three-fourths of Korean businesses in the Los Angeles are located outside the enclave economy in the general market (Bonacich and Jung, 1982). Hannerz (1974) argues the cause of the expansion of the enclave economy to the non-enclave economy is that "the protected market is vital only in the initial stages of [ethnic] business development" (p. 193). As the size of the economic niche in the communities is enlarged by the participation of a larger number of ethnic members, the niche becomes an export platform from which ethnic firms can expand because of limited opportunity in the enclave economy (Waldinger, 1986: 259-261).

Light and his colleague (Light and Karageorgis, 1994; Light et al., 1994; Light et al., 1993) widen the horizon of ethnic entrepreneurship in this respect by arguing that not only is there entrepreneurship in the enclave economy, but entrepreneurship run by an ethnic group in the general market also should be considered as ethnic entrepreneurship. They call these immigrant economies both in the enclave and non-enclave as "ethnic economy."

On the other hand, the theory of opportunity structure explains ethnic entrepreneurship beyond the enclave economy theory. The opportunity structure in the general market is established with two characteristics: "low economies of scale" and "instability and uncertainty" (Waldinger, 1986; Waldinger et al., 1990). The low economies of scale refers to the absence of capital-intensive and high-volume competitors (Aldrich and Waldinger, 1990). Within low scale industry, immigrant entrepreneurs can successfully pursue a strategy of self-exploitation, and the entry of immigrants as entrepreneurs is relatively easier than in the general market due to less competition with large capitalists. Examples of small-scale industries are taxi drivers and inner-city small shops such as Korean immigrant entrepreneurs in the Los Angeles area (Bonacich and Jung, 1982). To keep the cost low, the entrepreneurs in the low scale economy tend to work long hours, exploit unpaid family labor, and use cheap ethnic laborers.

Another opportunity structure arises when the economic structure is characterized by instability and uncertainty. The structure emerges when demand for products is unstable and when production has limited possibilities for the technique of mass manufacturing on assembly lines (Waldinger, 1986). While staple products are handled by large-scale and capital intensive firms, the products with unstable demand and limited opportunity for mass production are left for small-scale firms, catering to an unpredictable and/or fluctuating demand (Aldrich and Waldinger, 1990: 117). Thus, in these industries, there is little expectation of competition between large- and small-scale firms.

Garment industries in Paris, London, and New York have been observed as examples of industries that are dominated by small immigrant firms in which immigrants take advantage of the nature of the opportunity structure in the industry (Morokvasic et al., 1990). The garment industry is a feasible example in that demand for products is unstable and the process of production does not fit into the techniques of mass production and mass distribution because of fast changes in fashions. Therefore, the garment industry is left without being occupied by large capitalists, providing opportunities for small immigrant firms.

However, because Waldinger (1986) and his colleagues (Aldrich and Waldinger, 1990; Morokvasic et al., 1990; Waldinger et al., 1990) focus mainly on the opportunity structures in the economy of which immigrants can make use, they tend to underestimate ethnic resources and cultural traits as much as cultural theory tends to overemphasize them. As a consequence of the underestimation of ethnic resources, the theory of opportunity structure places too little concern on two aspects: individual resources such as human capital and capacity and/or methods to mobilize resources; and group resources, such as networks and ethnic resources, that become crucial for both establishment and management. In addition, opportunity structure theory regards these two resources as only useful for business maintenance, disregarding their important roles in business establishment.

They also tend to roughly speculate that the structure of immigrant entrepreneurship is first founded in the enclave and then expanded to the larger market. Based on the history of the establishment of the Atlanta Korean community, however, a few Korean entrepreneurs started from the economic niche outside the enclave, when there was no enclave economy and the Korean population in Atlanta was small. After Korean entrepreneurship in Atlanta was somewhat developed, the patterns develop that some Korean immigrants directly jumped into the general non-enclave market for entrepreneurship and others established themselves in the enclave. This induced the emergence of the two economic niches at the same time and indicates that an enclave economy is not a necessary prerequisite for the expansion of immigrant entrepreneurship to the general market.

MULTIPLE CAUSATION OF IMMIGRANT ENTREPRENEURSHIP

Structural theory views ethnic entrepreneurship from a wide perspective in the sense that it attempts to determine the position of ethnic enterprises in the whole economic structure. On the other hand, reactive cultural theory allows for the examination of the reasons why there is a differential rate of participation in entrepreneurship among different disadvantaged groups. In addition, network theories provide perspectives in rather smaller unite to show in the community how members are interrelated to generate resources necessary for immigrant entrepreneurship. However, as indicated early in this chapter, immigrant entrepreneurship is not an outcome of one or two factors. Rather, it is influenced by multiple factors to make immigrant entrepreneurship possible, such as networks, structural factors, and cultural or ethnic resources, which simultaneously influence immigrants and encourage an entrepreneurial environment to emerge in the immigrant community.

There are structural disadvantages in the labor market that are caused by discrimination and insufficient English skills and that, in turn, compel immigrants to go into entrepreneurship; there are structural advantages such as available and/or captive markets in the inner city neighborhoods and the enclave economy that provide opportunities for immigrants to enter into entrepreneurship; there are personal advantages such as family networks, social networks, and higher educational background that empower immigrants with competitive advantages to pursue entrepreneurship; and there are ethnic resources such as rotating credit associations, a hard working work ethic, a frugal attitude, and a source of unpaid family labor or reliable coethnic labor that provide immigrants with advantages for entrepreneurship despite of harsh working environments.

The disadvantages cultivate a reactive solidarity in the ethnic community. The solidarity enables community members to forge strong ties among coethnic members, which later develop networks in the community. Thus networks, in turn, generate resources which ultimately transform the environment into a favorable one for the establishment of entrepreneurship.

The networks are major assets for resource mobilization and allocation of economic pursuits in entrepreneurship. Accordingly, entrepreneurship must be comprehended through networks by which the immigrants gain information, resources, and social support, because networks are the most prominent source of resource mobilization for the economic pursuits of immigrants. Although the vast majority of network theories focus on how networks are established between the people of sending countries and of receiving countries, influencing an increase in the immigration rate, they focus less on how networks are established after arriving in a new country. As a result, although network theories recognize the importance of networks in economic pursuits after immigration, the fragmentary understanding of networks after immigration has a shortcoming in explaining how immigrant entrepreneurs utilize social networks in the immigrant community and, ultimately gain resources necessary for business establishment.

Moreover, network theory assumes that networks are equally available to everyone in the community as soon as immigrants get into the ethnic community after immigration. However, there is a variety of networks in immigrant communities and the difference in the context of networks provides immigrants with different advantages in the pursuit of entrepreneurship. Overlooking this difference in networks, some network theorists tend to contemplate the two components of networks—family networks and social networks—in one concept of network ties, while others examine only one side of networks. Some researchers misinterpret social networks as ethnic resources in the community. Therefore, individual networks should be perceived in the way in which they operate to generate resources on the basis of the types of networks—family networks or social networks.

Further, networks in the coethnic community ensure access to capital, a labor supply, and updated business information (Werbner, 1987) and relationships in the ethnic community reinforce and reaffirm the stability and extent of networks (Massey et al., 1987: chapter 6; Werbner, 1984). Therefore, regardless of how much these networks are crucial for resource mobilization for entrepreneurship, the causation between networks and the emergence of ethnic entrepreneurship should be explained by simultaneous consideration of individual advantages such as ethnic and/or class resources and structural factors.

However, it is important to examine these resources on the basis of how and at which stages of business establishment and management they are utilized. Theories of ethnic entrepreneurship not only tend to consider each resource separately, but they also tend to assume all these resources are utilized in all stages of businesses. However, each resource has different merits and advantages and is utilized in different stages of business establishment and operation. That is, certain resources are more useful for business establishment and others for business management. Thus, these resources should be contemplated according to their usefulness at each stage.

In addition, class resources need to be considered simultaneously with networks and ethnic resources. Inasmuch as ethnic resources are important for ethnic entrepreneurship, class resources such as entrepreneurial motivations, capacity of organization, or financial and human capital are fundamental elements for ethnic businesses where immigrants are essentially in a disadvantaged situation. For instance, class resources, which are in most cases measured by educational level, are largely recognized as a favorable factor and have a positive influence for immigrant entrepreneurship. However, previous studies do not demonstrate the direct impact of class resources, and overlook how educational background is capitalized to generate resources necessary to establish or manage ethnic businesses. In this study, however, class resources measured by educational level will be examined to uncover how educational level is converted into favorable resources for immigrant entrepreneurship. To uncover this connection, educational level will be examined in conjunction with social networks. Social networks tend to reflect the socio-economic background and status of immigrants in the country of origin. Therefore, educational background should be examined simultaneously with social networks to find out the impact of high educational level on immigrant entrepreneurship.

Structural theory, on the other hand, fails to examine how disadvantages in the labor market and advantages of the structural gap become effective in the entrepreneurial environment. That is, although structural theory recognizes a structural gap in the mainstream economy and the enclave economy in the coethnic community, that provides opportunities for immigrants to utilize for business establishments, it does not take full consideration of how immigrants utilize those factors and how they are combined with immigrants' individual advantages such as educational background, ethnic and/or class resources, and networks. Given the structural advantage that is available for all disadvantaged minorities and immigrants, structural theory does not explain why not all disadvantaged groups utilize the structural advantages to achieve economic mobility. As a result, structural theory cannot explain why certain immigrant groups are more successful in establishing entrepreneurship resulting in differences in the rate of entrepreneurship among different ethnic and immigrant groups. Therefore, whether structural factors work in a favorable way also should be examined in conjunction with such individual resources as utilization of social networks, class resources, and ethnic resources.

In conclusion, ethnic entrepreneurship, particularly immigrant entrepreneurship, is not a consequence of a single factor. It requires various factors from the structural level (i.e., ethnic resources, and economic niches) to the individual level (i.e., educational level and networks). Furthermore, all these factors are intertwined to make immigrant entrepreneurship possible, and differences in the possession of resources lead immigrant entrepreneurs to different pathways into the enclave or non-enclave economy on the basis of the resources that they can generate. Therefore, immigrant entrepreneurship should be contemplated by taking into consideration of all these factors simultaneously to uncover dynamics of ethnic entrepreneurship in the general economy.

CHAPTER III

Data, Methods, and Research Questions

Since entrepreneurship is one of the most prominent occupations for Korean immigrants, data have been collected by interviewing Korean entrepreneurs in Atlanta. Since interviewees reveal that first generation Korean immigrants seem to perceive entrepreneurship as the only alternative for economic mobility, the data are examined to provide information on how such a high proportion of Korean immigrants enter entrepreneurship and what kinds of processes they undergo to become entrepreneurs. The study of Korean entrepreneurship in Atlanta is especially valuable since the community has recently expanded to its current size, which allows us to investigate the dynamics of network establishment and resource mobilization.

KOREAN COMMUNITY IN ATLANTA

The size of the Korean community in Atlanta has grown very rapidly since the late 1980s. Table 3-1 shows the traits of Koreans in Georgia and Table 3-2 shows the traits of Korean businesses in the Atlanta MSA. Since most of the Korean population in Georgia lives in the Atlanta MSA, we can extrapolate the general traits of the Koreans in Atlanta from that of the Korean population in Georgia. Min (1983) estimated the total number of Korean families in Atlanta including Korean-American interracial families at 725, and the total number of Korean families engaged in business at 283. If we calculate approximately, assuming that there are five members in each family

Table 3-1: Demographics and Economic Characteristics of Koreans in Georgia (%)

	Georgia
Total Number of Koreans (N)	14,432
Foreign-Born (in Korea)	80.9
Age	
Under 18 yrs	26.8
18 to 39 yrs	44.9
40 to 59 yrs	23.8
60 to 74 yrs	3.7
75 yrs and over	0.7
Educational Attainment	
Persons 18 years and over (N)	10,562
Less than 5th grade	4.1
5th to 12th grade (no diploma)	15.8
High School (include equivalency)	31.7
Some college or associate degree	21.0
Bachelor's degree	15.8
Graduate or professional degree	8.2
Income in 1989	
Households (N)	3,396
Less than $10,000	14.6
$10,000 to $24,999	30.2
$25,000 to $49,999	34.1
$50,000 to $99,999	16.4
$100,000 or more	4.7
Median ($)	28,234
Mean ($)	39,099
Class of Worker	
Employed persons 16 years and over (N)	6,598
Private wage and salary workers	72.2
Local government workers	1.3
State government workers	2.7
Federal government workers	3.9
Self-employed workers	16.9
Unpaid family workers	3.1

Table 3-1 (continued)

Industry	
Employed persons 16 years and over (N)	6,298
Agriculture, forestry, and fisheries	0.3
Mining	0.0
Construction	2.4
Manufacturing	13.8
Transportation	2.4
Communication and other public utilities	0.7
Wholesale trade	4.2
Retail trade	40.0
Service industry [1]	26.0
Professional and related services	16.0
Public administration	1.9
Residence in 1985	
Persons 5 years and over (N)	13,232
Same house	29.2
Different house in Georgia	24.7
Different house in other states	18.6
Elsewhere	27.5

* indicates no one in the category.

[1] Banking and credit agencies; Insurance, real-estate, and other finance;
   Business and repair services; Private households; Other personal services;
   Entertainment and recreation services.

Sources: U.S. Department of Commerce. Bureau of the Census. *Census of
   Population and Housing: Georgia* Washington, D.C.: GPO 1910-1960;
   ibid. *Census of Population, General Population Characteristics:
   Metropolitan Areas* Washington, D.C.: GPO 1990.

Table 3-2: Traits of Korean-Owned Firms in the Atlanta MSA

	Atlanta Metropolitan Area
1992	
All Firms (Korean-Owned)	
Firms (N)	2,338
Sales & Receipts ($1,000)	262,310
Firms with Paid Employees (Korean-Owned)	
Firms (N)	582
Employees (N)	2,156
Sales & Receipts ($1,000)	184,938
Annual Payroll ($1,000)	22,122
1987	
All Firms (Korean-Owned)	
Firms (N)	1,266
Sales and Receipts ($1,000)	127,739
Firms with Paid Employees (Korean-Owned)	
Firms (N)	462
Employees (N)	1,130
Sales and Receipts ($1,000)	96,531
Annual Payroll ($1,000)	10,270

Sources: U.S. Department of Commerce. Bureau of the Census. *Census of Population and Housing, Supplementary Reports about Metropolitan Areas* Washington, D.C.: GPO 1990; ibid. *Economic Census, Survey of Minority-Owned Business Enterprises: Asian Americans, American Indians, and Other Minorities* Washington, D.C.: GPO 1992; ibid. *Economic Census, Survey of Minority-Owned Business Enterprises: Asian Americans, American Indians, and Other Minorities* Washington, D.C.: GPO 1987.

(i.e., a couple, two children, and possibly one extended family), the total number of Koreans in Atlanta becomes about 3,600 persons in 1983.

According to the 1990 Census, however, the Korean population in the Atlanta Metropolitan Statistical Area (MSA) had increased to 10,120 persons. Moreover, at the time of my data collection in 1994, the Korean community organization argued that the actual number of Korean immigrants in Atlanta is much larger because the Census did not account for the massive influx of the Korean population into Atlanta after the Census. A Korean community organization estimated that the number of Koreans in Atlanta MSA was about 40,000 in 1994. Since a large number of Korean immigrants moved to Atlanta recently from other cities in the U.S. or immigrated directly from Korea to Atlanta, the size of the community has grown drastically, and so has the number of Korean businesses. As Table 3-2 shows, Korean-owned firms in 1992 increased two fold since 1987 and more than eight fold since Min's study in 1983.

In addition, the data I collected in Atlanta support the estimate of the community organization in that 76.1% of interviewees in my data have lived elsewhere in the U.S. and moved recently to Atlanta for a variety of reasons. Atlanta is seen as a good place to start a business, with a growing economy, friendly business environment, and low start-up costs compared to other major metropolitan areas. These expectations were heightened by the 1996 Olympics in Atlanta.

Recent Korean immigrants have come to Los Angeles, New York, or Chicago, where Korean communities have been established for a long time, to assimilate or be absorbed into an already existing social structure in the Korean communities. However, unlike Korean immigrants in the other larger cities, Korean immigrants in Atlanta have had to establish a new community, because the Atlanta Korean community was quite small and expanded rapidly only recently, as a consequence of the migration of Korean immigrants from other cities. Since the Atlanta Korean community is new, patterns of searching for occupational or business opportunities are expected to be different from the patterns in the larger cities where the history of Korean communities is relatively longer, and the ways for Korean immigrants to get into the community are already established.

Therefore, due to the short history of the Korean community in Atlanta, the study can provide new perspectives on the ways in which

Korean immigrants procure access to occupational and business opportunities.

DATA/METHODS

Data

In the Korean ethnic economy, businesses can be divided into two sets on the basis of ethnicity of clientele: one in the enclave economy, catering mainly to Korean customers; the other outside the enclave economy, catering to non-Korean customers. The line is drawn between the enclave and non-enclave businesses on the basis of the ratio of Korean customers. Businesses with Koreans as over 50% of the major customers are included in the enclave economy. Businesses with Koreans as less than 50% of the major customers are included in the non-enclave.

The division of economic niches is based on the theory of the enclave economy. Portes and Manning (1986) argue that the enclave economy is dependent on three characteristics: availability of sources of capital; existence of a substantial number of immigrants with entrepreneurial experiences; and the availability of sources of cheap coethnic labor. Enclave economy theory also relies on the assumption that coethnic customers live in a concentrated area around the enclave economy. Since the major assumption of enclave theory is that immigrant entrepreneurship is highly dependent on coethnic clients, the ethnicity of customers is the defining factor of the enclave economy.

However, although the Korean enclave economy does rely on Korean customers, there is no tendency that Korean immigrants in Atlanta are concentrated in a particular residential area. According to the 1990 Census Tracts, Koreans are neither concentrated in areas where the enclave nor non-enclave economies are established. Table 3-3 shows the ethnicity of residents around the enclave and the non-enclave economies; the non-enclave data are given for the largest block selected for a block sampling at the Five-Points area of downtown Atlanta (See the section Sampling in this chapter). The table allows us to speculate how insignificantly Korean immigrant entrepreneurs rely on residents around the enclave economy. It also shows how insignificantly Korean enterprises in the non-enclave, selected by block sampling, rely on African-American residents near the businesses.

Table 3-3: Ethnic Composition of Residents in the Enclave and the Non-Enclave Economy

	Enclave Economy	Non-Enclave Economy
Total Number of Residents	60,985	162
White	43,870	82
Black	10,778	73
American Indian	168	1
Chinese	664	6
Filipino	91	-
Japanese	157	-
Asian Indian	607	-
Korean	641	-
Other Asians	1,431	-
Hispanic	5,292	2
Other	2,555	-

Sources: U.S. Department of Commerce. Bureau of the Census. *Census of Population and Housing, Population and Housing Characteristics for Census Tracts and Block Numbering Areas, Atlanta, GA MSA* Washington, D.C.: GPO 1990.

Unlike the argument of enclave theory that the enclave economy relies on ethnic residential concentration around the economy, only 641 Koreans live in the enclave area, where the largest number of the enclave businesses catering to Korean customers is concentrated. Since the Korean residential areas are scattered in the Atlanta MSA, it is impossible to identify the enclave economy on the basis of residential areas where Koreans are concentrated. Moreover, with regard to the non-enclave economy at the Five Points area, the non-enclave Korean businesses cannot be identified on the basis of the ethnicity of residents around the area, because the non-Korean customers also do not live near the Korean businesses.

Therefore, it is not plausible to sample Korean businesses neither in the enclave nor outside it on the basis of ethnic composition of residents, since the residents around Korean businesses are not the major customers of the businesses. Furthermore, except for the businesses selected by block sampling, most non-enclave Korean businesses are scattered in the inner city residential areas. As a result, it is impossible to select the non-enclave Korean businesses in relation to the location of the businesses and the race/ethnicity of residences around the ethnic economy. Accordingly, the division of the economy between the enclave and the non-enclave on the basis of the ethnicity of the clientele is the most plausible definition for this study.

Table 3-4 shows the number of businesses owned by Korean immigrants in the Atlanta area and the number of Korean businesses interviewed on the basis of types of businesses. Although business types in the non-enclave economy vary, groceries catering to inner city African-American neighborhoods are the single most predominant business type, followed by liquor stores and coin laundry/dry cleaning. Other businesses outside the enclave economy include stores for general merchandise, wigs, beauty supplies, clothing, or fast food. Although most non-enclave businesses are either scattered in the inner city neighborhoods or clustered at the Five Points area of Atlanta's downtown, waiting on African American customers, dry cleaning stores are located mostly in suburban middle class neighborhoods.

On the other hand, businesses in the enclave economy provide cultural products such as Korean foods and groceries, or seasonings imported from Korea, and Korean restaurants with traditional foods. Restaurants are the most pervasive type of business in the enclave economy, catering mainly to a Korean clientele. As was indicated earlier, the size of the community drastically enlarged recently; therefore, the number of businesses in the service sector such as travel agencies, real estate and insurance agencies, building construction and interior design, and law and accounting offices has also grown drastically.

Ethnic entrepreneurship has been typically considered as small retail stores, and most studies of ethnic entrepreneurship have overlooked the service sector operated by ethnic entrepreneurs catering to coethnic communities. However, an inclusion of the service sector of the enclave economy in the data paints a different picture than the typical conception of ethnic entrepreneurship, since these businesses do not require as much financial capital as retail stores, and owners of these businesses tend to have a higher educational background.

As the size of the Korean community grew drastically, there also grew a great demand for professional assistance from doctors, lawyers, accountants, and insurance or real estate agents. The increased demand in the service sector is because Korean immigrants usually encounter a language barrier and an unfamiliar legal system when it comes time for them to establish their own businesses. These professional services

Table 3-4: Businesses Owned by Koreans in the Atlanta Area

	Businesses Counted in Atlanta[1]	Businesses Interviewed	Rejected, Closed or Moved
Enclave Businesses			
Professionals & semi-professionals [2]	92	10.7%	5
Service businesses [3]	220	18.2%	8
Retail stores	31	5.0%	3
Restaurants & grocery [5]	62	5.7%	2
Wholesales	59	4.4%	6
Non-Enclave Businesses			
Groceries	291	11.3%	11
Liquor stores	80	3.1%	3
Dry cleaning and coin laundry	130	6.3%	1
Retail businesses [6]	98	17.6%	1
Wholesales *	0	4.4%	4
Service businesses [7] *	0	10.7%	0
Doctors *	0	2.5%	0
Total	1,063	159	44

[1] 1994 to November, 1994 during the data collection period.

[2] Professionals & semi-professionals include doctors, lawyers, accountants, pharmacists, Oriental medical doctors, and private teaching institutions such as musical instruments or martial arts.

[3] Service sectors include beauty salons, auto body or repair shops, insurance and real estate agencies, travel agencies, shipping companies, and Korean video rental shops.

[4] Retail stores include gift shops, health food stores, Korean bakeries, and clothing stores.

[5] Restaurants & grocery includes Korean food restaurants, Korean-Chinese food restaurants, Korean-Japanese restaurants, and Korean grocery stores.

[6] Retail businesses include jewelry stores, wig stores, general merchandise stores, beauty supply stores, clothing stores, and furniture stores.

[7] Service sectors include electronic repairs, jewelry repairs, printing, building maintenance, fast food stores, and convenience stores.

* The three business were counted as 0, because Wholesales and Doctors are classified as enclave businesses, selecting them through the list of the enclave businesses, and because Service businesses were not expected in the non-enclave (There will be a further explanation in the section of Sampling).

meet their desperate need for help. In addition, as the number of new businesses increases, there is a greater demand for construction and interior design companies and wholesalers that sell equipment necessary for business operations. Therefore, the demand opens up opportunities for professionals such as doctors, lawyers, accountants, or other businesses to cater solely to Korean clientele.

The number of retail businesses in the non-enclave has been counted by selecting five different blocks. The largest block is in the Five Points area of downtown Atlanta. The rest of the blocks selected were in inner city neighborhoods. The businesses counted by block sampling include not only retail businesses, but also service businesses such as fast food stores, painting, or printing. Although the total number of service businesses in the non-enclave was not counted, quite a few Korean entrepreneurs operate services such as fast food outlets and convenience stores. In addition, despite the fact that doctors were counted as professionals in the enclave businesses because they advertise in Korean community newspapers, they tend to have more white customers than Koreans. As a result, they are included in the non-enclave economy in the data.

Sampling

Sampling is under three schemes for businesses in the enclave and non-enclave. Businesses in the enclave are selected randomly from a list developed based on advertisements in three Korean community newspapers. The list includes only businesses which advertised three consecutive times, because active advertisements indicate that the businesses are currently actively operated. There are two rationales for identifying the enclave businesses by advertisements. One is that since the newspapers are printed in Korean, the advertisements are presumed to be aimed at Korean customers. Also, since the newspapers are solely run by fees from advertisements and distributed free to readers, and above all since the rate for advertisements is very cheap, business owners expecting Korean customers would actively advertise their businesses in them. The cheap price of advertising insures inclusion of most enclave businesses.

Most businesses outside the enclave economy are selected randomly, based on lists provided by business associations, and the rest were selected by block sampling for businesses without associations. I obtained the list of businesses catering to non-Korean customers from the presidents of the business associations. The most numerous businesses such as groceries, liquor stores, and dry cleaning/coin laundry stores have business associations, which provide lists of businesses of these kinds in Atlanta. The businesses tend to be geographically scattered, and located near residential areas. The lists of businesses provided by associations are expected to include the majority of businesses, because the associations provide benefits by furnishing businesses with information, purchasing products in a large quantity with better deals than can be attained through individual purchases, and taking collective action against government officials whenever necessary, such as securing businesses from crime. These businesses are geographically scattered around inner city neighborhoods and middle class neighborhoods, where random sampling from the lists is most appropriate.

However, other than the businesses with associations, those without associations tend to be clustered in the Five Points area of downtown Atlanta or clustered on large streets where there is heavy passer-by traffic. Figure 3-1 is a map that shows the clusters of businesses in the Five Points area and in the enclave. Retail stores in the non-enclave are mostly selected by block sampling, because they tend to be geographically concentrated without business associations. These businesses were selected through block sampling. Four different blocks in residential areas and in the Five Points area were selected for block sampling. Although block sampling was used to select mostly retail stores, other kinds of businesses on the blocks selected, such as service businesses, were interviewed as well.

Unexpectedly, there were changes in business categories across the economic niches, and the emergence of a new business category. Although Wholesalers and some Korean doctors in the non-enclave economy advertised in Korean newspapers and were initially selected as enclave businesses, they turned out to have more non-Korean customers. Thus, if they were found to have more non-Korean customers in the course of the interview, they were included in the non-enclave businesses in the analysis, disregarding their initial categorization.

In addition, the presence of service businesses in the non-enclave economy (i.e., printing stores, repair stores, fast food stores, and convenience stores) was unexpected until I selected and counted the businesses on the blocks. In the process of counting businesses in the

Figure 3-1: Map of Clusters of Businesses in the Enclave and Non-Enclave of the Atlanta MSA

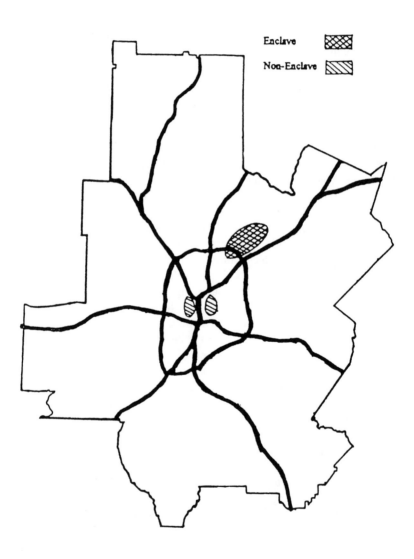

selected blocks, I realized the number of service businesses, catering to non-Korean customers was a significant portion of the block sample. Due both to the unexpected shifts of economic niches of some businesses (Wholesalers and Doctors) to the non-enclave, and the emergence of unexpected business types (Service businesses) in the non-enclave, such businesses in the non-enclave economy were initially not counted, but classified as non-enclave businesses later.

Data Collection

I have collected data through face-to-face interviews with 159 Korean entrepreneurs who owned businesses in the Atlanta Metropolitan Area from April to November of 1994. The interviews were conducted in Korean based on a structured questionnaire (see Appendix A). Some entrepreneurs refused to sign consent form (Yoo, 1996: Appendix A), because they worried about signing a document in English without knowing its content. Although I explained that the purpose of signing the consent form was to protect the rights of interviewees, they refused to sign and I could get the consent form signed by only about half of the interviewees. For the interviewees who refused to sign, I gave them a copy of the consent form, so that they could contact me in the future if they had questions about the survey or interviews.

I recorded answers by hand, while interviewees responded to my questions. Because the questionnaire was in English and the interviewees were uncomfortable with English, I asked questions in Korean and recorded their answers in English by hand. Because of the characteristics of the questionnaire, with two thirds of the questions open-ended, it was not desirable to have mail surveys. Five questionnaires were experimentally left with interviewees either because they did not have time at the moment or because they were not at the business when I visited. None of these questionnaires was returned to me. Consequently, all interviews were conducted face-to-face. During interviews, whenever issues occurred, about which the questionnaire did not include questions, I asked follow-up questions. However, I did not have any follow-up interviews after finishing the data collection.

All interviews were conducted at the businesses during business hours. In that way, I could observe business operations, the race composition of customers, and the size of the businesses. Only one interview was conducted outside the business, because the entrepreneur preferred to be interviewed in a place separate from his employees. Most interviewees were phoned to make appointments before going to their businesses for an interview. Due to unfamiliarity of my identity in the community, appointments were important because it helped to reduce reluctance of being interviewed. If it were not for the appointments, the rejection rate would have been higher.

I selected blocks according to directions from business owners at other places, who told me several blocks in which Korean businesses are highly concentrated. When I arrived at the blocks selected, I first identified all of the Korean-owned businesses on the block. I then requested an interview from each of the business owners.

Especially for the block samples, it was important to be introduced to other entrepreneurs by an entrepreneur who had already been interviewed. The entrepreneurs who already had been interviewed introduced me to other owners in the block. Since the other entrepreneurs could trust my identity based on the trust of the entrepreneur already interviewed, they tended to readily agree to interviews. If interviewees did not know the owner of any other businesses on the block, they at least helped to identify locations of other businesses.

The initial interview target was 200; however, the number was reduced to 159. Out of 203 entrepreneurs contacted, I was unable to interview 44 (21.7%) entrepreneurs because they refused, had closed, or moved (see Table 3-4). The major reason that entrepreneurs declined interviews was reluctance to be questioned about financial issues. Six interviewees refused to answer questions about annual gross sales, and thirteen about money invested in the current businesses. Although some interviewees seemed uncomfortable talking about their financial condition with a stranger, most were quite willing to give financial information during the interview.

Interviewees were also reluctant to answer questions about inter-racial problems (i.e., the relationship between Korean merchants and black customers). Also, some owners on the lists of business associations were not in the business any longer and ownership had changed. When I called on appointments, I asked for owners by name. However, when the business owners had changed, the new owners refused to be interviewed. When females answered the phone, they were most likely to refuse to be interviewed. The persons who answered the phone seemed to be wives of the shop owners, judging by their ages and the authoritative tone of their voices. When young women answered the phone, they most likely asked me to wait and let me talk to the owners. Considering their younger ages, I assumed they might have been employees or children of the owners.

Seven interviews were conducted over the phone, because I could not make appointments with the entrepreneurs due to their busy schedules, because they preferred to be interviewed over the phone, or because they had time to be interviewed at the moment. Also, I had a difficulty locating eight businesses, because some are located right next to the inner city residential area, and there were no street signs to find the businesses. I did not interview the owners of eight businesses that I could not locate.

Since I was a stranger to Korean immigrants in the Atlanta community, two interviewees were suspicious of my identification at the beginning of interviews. When it came to the financial questions, the two interviewees asked me to show them some identification. After examining my student identification and driver's license, they became friendly and willing to answer questions. However, most interviewees were very cooperative and willing to answer questions, although a couple of interviewees avoided answering any questions related to finances.

Face-to-face interview was the most appropriate method for collecting data, since this study requires information about entrepreneurs' personal experiences (i.e., prior employment experiences, ethnicity of the employers at the prior employment, sources of resource mobilization, ways of entry into entrepreneurship, and factors influencing occupancy of the economic niches). Although the most frequently used source of secondary data on immigrant entrepreneurs was the Census, the data are inappropriate to examine immigrant entrepreneurship because they do not include any of the information listed above.

METHODS

For an indepth comprehension of Korean businesses, most questions were analyzed using two methods: descriptive statistics and qualitative analysis. The descriptive statistics were used to analyze the general tendencies of the economic pursuits and entrepreneurial activities of Korean immigrants. Although this study is not designed to be a comparative study, information generated through statistics enables a further comparison with studies done in other cities (i.e., New York,

Los Angeles, or Chicago) with regard to entrepreneurial tendencies of Korean immigrants in the United States.

On the other hand, the text of open-ended questions provides a rich content, supporting the general tendencies shown in the statistical data. For example, when interviewees were asked about their motivations for starting entrepreneurship with response categories (e.g., Appendix: Q 48), most people listed economic reasons as their major motivation. However, when they were asked the same question in an open-ended manner (e.g., Appendix: Q 35), interviewees revealed more personal experiences such as deficient language skills, limited opportunities in the labor market, and discrimination. Therefore, the combination of two methods made the data not only more reliable, but also richer in terms of the personal and psychological background that statistical data might miss.

KEY CONCEPTS

Prior Employment Experiences

Korean immigrants are divided into two groups in terms of occupational experience after immigration. Although some start businesses immediately after immigration, about 82.4% of the Korean immigrants interviewed have had employment experiences before their entry into entrepreneurship. Although the time of immigration has only a slight impact on the proportion of those with employment experiences, a lower proportion of the earlier immigrants have had prior employment experiences (78.6%), whereas the proportion is higher among the later immigrants (84.5%).

Based on whether or not Korean immigrants have had employment experiences, we can infer how many of them started entrepreneurship immediately after immigration. In other words, those without employment experiences are expected to start entrepreneurship not long after immigration, whereas those with employment experiences waited for a while to start entrepreneurship to collect business information or to save business capital. Therefore, those who started businesses without prior employment experiences are more successful.

In addition, the length of prior employment is also an indication of how the immigrants are successful in entering entrepreneurship. Since the majority of Korean immigrants perceive entrepreneurship as the only passage way for social mobility after immigration, they pursue entrepreneurship as quickly as possible after immigration. Thus, a shorter period of prior employment is one of the indications of successful entrepreneurs.

Earlier Immigrants vs. Later Immigrants

Earlier immigrants are those who came from 1965 to the 1979. Since the Immigration and Nationality Act Amendments of 1965, Korean immigration to the U.S. increased. Although some Koreans immigrated before 1965, the number is very small. Korean immigrants before 1965 were either political refugees at the turn of the century, war orphans, or Korean women who married American service men in Korea from the 1950s. Therefore, normal immigration did not start until the 1965 Amendments that prefer immigrants with professional backgrounds rather than racial preferences. The flow of Korean immigrants with high professional or managerial backgrounds influenced by the 1965 Amendment Acts established large Korean immigrant communities, that enabled the subsequent immigration of Koreans without such high professional or managerial backgrounds.

A large portion of the later immigrants are chain-migrants. Chain-migration can begin only when there is a sufficient population of immigrants in the host society. The chain-migrants are those who immigrated with family networks with help from family members in the United States. As will be shown in Chapter 4, chain-migrants came under the family sponsored preference categories: married sons and daughters of U.S. citizens; spouses and unmarried sons and daughters of permanent resident aliens and their children; married sons and daughters of U.S. citizens and their spouses and children; and brothers and sisters of U.S. citizens and their spouses and children.

When earlier immigrants economically and socially settle down in the host society, a tendency of chain-migration emerges since family or relatives of earlier immigrants tend to immigrate based on their connection to others in the host society. Although not all Korean immigrants who came from 1980 to 1994 are chain-migrants, chain-migrants make up a large portion of the recent immigrants (e.g., 55.3% of the interviewees in my data are chain-migrants). If it is not a direct family chain-migration, some are encouraged to immigrate from information provided by friends.

Family Networks

Samples are analyzed based on the possession of family networks. As indicated above, chain-migrants are those with family members already in America. There was a tendency from the late 1970s that a large number of Korean immigrants came to the United States with the help of family members who were already U.S. citizens or residents. Korean immigrants, who came with the help of their family members in the United States, immigrated with family networks already established before immigration. Chain-migration is perceived to be utterly advantageous for immigrants, who are not familiar with the new society, to settle down and have a better chance for economic success.

Therefore, network theory strongly argues that help from family members, who have been in the U.S. for a long period, is a strong resource for immigrants' economic pursuits. Family networks are especially advantageous resources for newcomers to search for jobs, to find housing, or to establish future businesses. Since newcomers are not familiar with the host society, they need substantial help from those who immigrated earlier and know more about the U.S. society. As a result, those with family networks are expected to find jobs with higher wages or prestige or to become entrepreneurs in a shorter period. These family networks are systematically examined in this study to find out how helpful family networks are for newcomers to find jobs and to establish businesses quickly after immigration.

Social Networks

Unlike family networks, most social networks are established after immigration. After immigration, almost all Korean immigrants are introduced to the community members, some by the help of family and friends or some by their own efforts. Since social networks tend to reflect socio-economic background from the country of origin, the characteristics of social networks that Korean immigrants establish after immigration might differ based on their backgrounds, and the resources generated by the networks also differ, as a result. Therefore, social networks are examined to find out how Korean immigrants with different backgrounds in Korea establish social networks differently, and how different social networks generate various resources that ultimately provide advantages for business establishment.

Most importantly, this study systematically examines how family networks and social networks operate differently and are used for different purposes. By examining differences in the two kinds of networks, we can assess which networks are crucial to Korean entrepreneurship.

Class Resources

Class resources are measured by educational level. This study uncovers how educational level is capitalized to be favorable for immigrant entrepreneurship. Although class resources are largely recognized as a positive influence on immigrant entrepreneurship, researchers do not indicate the direct impact of class resources. To find this out, this study examines educational level in conjunction with social networks. Social networks tend to reflect the socio-economic background and status of immigrants in the country of origin. Therefore, educational background as a class resource is examined simultaneously with social networks to find out the impact of educational background on immigrant entrepreneurship.

Ethnic Resources

Ethnic resources have been considered as cultural resources. Regardless of terms, ethnic resource tend to indicate values, attitudes, or material resources that immigrants brought from their country of origin. Unlike class resources that are selectively available for those with higher educational backgrounds, ethnic resources tend to be available rather equally for all members in an immigrant community. Ethnic resources include cheap labor from coethnic members, willingness to work long hours, unpaid family labor, and rotating credit associations (RCA). A pervasive perception is that ethnic entrepreneurs have the advantage of a source of cheap labor in coethnic members. The new arrivals look for job opportunities in the enclave labor market and become a source of cheap labor. In addition, immigrant entrepreneurs are known as hard workers. They tend to work for much longer hours than native entrepreneurs. The cultural background of hard work thus becomes a valuable resource for ethnic entrepreneurs.

Furthermore, immigrant entrepreneurs utilize unpaid family labor as a labor source. They utilize the family labor not only because the entrepreneurs trust them more, but also the labor force gives immigrant entrepreneurs a competitive edge. Rotating credit associations (RCA: Kye) has long been considered to be a strong advantage of immigrant entrepreneurs, a source of income that native entrepreneurs do not have and that is known to provide capital resources for business establishment. These ethnic resources will be examined to find out how they are useful for the ethnic entrepreneurship.

Resource Mobilization

Resources are examined on the basis of capacities for capital provision and information collection through family networks and social networks. When Koreans immigrate to the United States, they encounter a different social system. This unfamiliarity is the biggest barrier for immigrants to overcome. Moreover, insufficient language skills further prevent immigrants from acquiring information about the host society. As a consequence, Korean immigrants vigorously utilize and mobilize available sources to obtain social and economic mobility in the new society. Networks are one of the resources to be examined to find out how they are utilized for resource mobilization.

Family networks are an initial resource that Korean immigrants actively utilize to settle down after immigration. Family networks not only provide information about prospects for living in the United States before immigration, they also provide information about job opportunities and economic mobility through entrepreneurship. Family networks also help to expand further networks after immigration.

The expanded networks are social networks, which are established after immigration. Social networks constitute another crucial resource that influences the lives and economic pursuits of Korean immigrants. This is because social networks provide Korean immigrants with broader information on how immigrants can achieve economic mobility. Since the most important resources necessary to establish businesses are information and capital, social networks are examined to determine how the networks might generate these resources differently from family networks in pursuit of entrepreneurship.

Occupancy of Economic Niches

A comparison between the two economic niches, the enclave and non-enclave, reveals that more Korean immigrant entrepreneurs in Atlanta seem to engage in the non-enclave businesses. To examine this tendency, the structural opportunities that give Korean immigrants an advantage are examined. Structural theory argues that Korean immigrants can get into businesses because of the existence of markets, which have either not been served due to low profit margins and high crime, or which are unable to be served due to the uniqueness of the cultural products. Therefore, it is necessary to examine entrepreneurs who are capable of taking advantage of the existing structural opportunities and how they enter either of the economic niches.

Another issue concerns the reason why Korean immigrant entrepreneurs diverge into two different economic niches. This issue is explained through resource mobilization capacity on the basis of class resources and networks. Ethnic resources also are taken into account to see if they allow Korean immigrants to become more competitive over other immigrants or other minorities, if possible.

CHAPTER IV

Korean Immigrants in the United States

Based on the data aggregated by the Immigration and Naturalization Service, this chapter examines trends in the number of Korean immigrants admitted, their occupational background before immigration, and their legal background for admission as immigrants.

IMMIGRATION LAWS WHICH INFLUENCED TRENDS OF KOREAN IMMIGRATIONS

The Immigration and Nationality Act Amendments of 1965 induced massive Korean immigration with entirely different demographic characteristics from the earlier years. The major cause of the rise in Korean immigration was that the Amendments eliminated preferences in countries of origin for immigrants. As data demonstrate in the later section of this chapter, the U.S. immigration laws are the principal factor in determining the demographics and profiles of immigrants over various periods of time.

The McCarran-Walter Immigration and Nationality Act of 1952 was the first law that allowed Asians to immigrate to the United States as legal immigrants other than political refugees, students, or laborers since the turn of the century.[2] The Act of 1952, however, still contained a discriminatory element in that it limited the number of Asians through a quota system, whereas the Act set no numeric limits on European immigration to the U.S.

Despite the rigid restriction against Asian immigrants until the Amendments of 1965 was issued, as many as 11,771 Korean children and women came to the U.S. between 1945 and 1965 (Hurh and Kim, 1980). Orphaned children came as "immediate relatives" and women as "spouses of U.S. citizens," both of which were not subject to the quota limitation. After World War II, many Korean students began coming to the U.S. until 1965. W. Kim (1971: 26) estimates that more than 6,000 Korean students came to the U.S. between 1944 and 1965. It may well be assumed that a large portion of these students changed their legal status from students to permanent residents.

The Immigration and Nationality Act Amendments of 1965 had two primary purposes that influenced mass immigration from many Asian countries, including from Korea: one was to admit more educated immigrants with special skills or professional knowledge and dissuade the uneducated and unskilled immigrants that had dominated previous periods of immigration; the other was that the Amendments created opportunities for family reunification as a humane purpose through the preference category of "immediate relatives."

The major characteristic of the Amendments was that they abolished the "national origins" quota system, thereby eliminating national origin, race, or ancestry as a basis for immigration to the United States. The national origins quota system was established to preserve the balance between the various ethnic elements in the American population (Rodino, 1968). The quota system, however, had been practiced in a discriminatory way, favoring Northern and Western Europeans over other ethnic groups.

Instead of the national origins quota system, the Amendments of 1965 establish the "categories of preference" system, which favored persons with special occupational skills, abilities, or training, needed in the United States. Another favorable categories, that benefit later Korean immigrants in the long run, were preferences for relatives of U.S. citizens and permanent resident aliens. These categories were established to allow the reunification of immigrants with immediate family members in the United States. It took three years for the Amendments of 1965 to go into a full effect, because of a transition period that lasted through June 30, 1968 (Rodino, 1968).

Nonetheless, the amendments still discriminated against people other than Europeans, in that the preference categories and the 20,000 per-country limit were not applied to "Western Hemisphere" immigration, but only to "Eastern Hemisphere." However, the Immigration and Nationality Act Amendments of 1976 began to apply the 20,000 per-country limit to both the Western Hemisphere and the Eastern Hemisphere.

Another law, which resulted in increased Korean immigration after 1989, was the Immigration Reform and Control Act of 1986 (IRCA) which allowed immigrants to transfer their status from temporary to permanent residents. The IRCA of 1986 was to be effective from 1989, and legalized aliens who had resided in the United States in an unlawful status since January 1, 1982. That is, aliens who had entered the United States illegally or as temporary visitors on or before this date and then exceeded their allowed terms to stay, were permitted to transfer their status to legal permanent residents. The Act influenced Korean illegal residents to change their status to legal permanent resident statuses from 1989 that shows an abrupt increase in the statistics.

CHARACTERISTICS OF KOREAN IMMIGRATION

Table 4-1 shows the number of Korean immigrants admitted each year. The effect of the Amendments of 1965 becomes visible from the late 1960s. "Status adjusted" indicates immigrants who entered the United States under a temporary visa such as visitors for pleasure, students, business-related visitors, workers and employees, and others or unknown. Later, they changed their status from temporary to permanent residents.

The total number admitted, regardless of whether they are new arrivals or status adjusted, doubled in 1969. After the sharp increase of Korean immigrants admitted in the late 1960s, the number of the immigrants steadily increased until the late 1980s and began to decrease from 1988. However, although the proportional increase was sharp from the late 1960s, the sheer number of Koreans admitted in each year was much greater from the 1970s until the mid-1980s. The Amendments of 1965 nevertheless seems to have had an immediate and tremendous impact on Koreans who were already in the United States. That is, the number who had adjusted their status from other temporary positions to permanent residents started drastically increasing after 1967.

The dramatic increase of Korean immigrants after the Amendments of 1965 was accompanied by an increase in other Asian immigrants. The Asian share of the total immigrants to the U.S. increased from the year 1966. Asians constitute around 7.7% of the total immigrants

Table 4-1: Korean immigrants admitted to the U.S.

Years Admitted	Total number Admitted	Status on New arrivals (%)	Admittance Status Adjusted (%)[1]
1960	1,507	90.1	9.9
1965	2,165	89.8	10.2
1970	9,314	77.7	22.3
1975	28,362	91.7	8.3
1980	32,320	90.9	9.1
1985	35,253	86.6	13.4
1990 [2]	32,301	80.4	19.6
1993	18,026	68.7	31.3

Source: U.S. Department of Justice. Immigration and Naturalization Service. *Annual Reports: Immigration and Naturalization Service*, 1966-1977; ibid. *Statistical Yearbook of the Immigration and Naturalization Service*, 1979-1993.

[1] Status Adjusted is the Korean immigrants who entered the U.S. under temporary visas and changed their statuses to permanent residents.

[2] Immigration Reform and Control Act of 1986 (IRCA) becomes effective in 1989 with 10,364 of Korean legalized immigrants: 2,004 in 1989; 2,753 in 1990; 4,890 in 1991; 640 in 1992; and 77 in 1993.

admitted between 1960 and 1965, whereas Europeans constitutes 43.9% in the same period.[3] From 1971, the composition of Asian immigrants slightly outnumbered that of Europeans: 26.0% were Europeans and 27.9% were Asians. In 1980, however, the composition of immigrants between Asians and Europeans was completely reversed: 44.5% were Asians and 13.6% were Europeans. In 1990, the Asian share decreased to 22.0%, with the Europeans share at 7.3%.

Table 4-1 also shows a considerable increase in the number of status adjusted persons from 1989 to 1991. The reason for this increase in the number of status adjusted immigrants was the IRCA in 1986, which became effective from 1989. As was illustrated earlier, the IRCA was designed to legalize illegal aliens in the United States. The number of status adjusted Koreans became the most significant from 1989 to the 1990s. It was in 1991 that the highest number of Koreans (4,890 persons) were legalized by IRCA.

Notwithstanding prior years, however, in the early 1990s, what kept the total number of Koreans admitted to such a consistent level are Koreans who are status adjusted instead of new arrivals. From 1989 to the 1990s, despite of the decrease in the number of new arrivals from Korea, the proportion of the status-adjusted Korean immigrants increases each year , which significantly contributed to the total number of Korean immigrants admitted.

Figure 4-1 presents trends of changes in the total number of Korean immigrants admitted. The total number of all immigrants admitted to the United States reached a peak in 1991. Unlike the tendency of decrease in the total number of all immigrants admitted to the United States from 1992, a trend of decline in number of Korean immigrants had already started in the late 1980s. Primarily, decreased new arrivals are the major influence for the decline in the total number of Koreans admitted in the 1990s.

The decrease in the number of Korean immigrants from the late 1980s is a result of the diminished number of new arrivals, which indicates a decreased interests in immigration to the U.S. among Koreans. This reduced attraction for immigration accompanied by rapid economic development in Korea from the late 1980s, which indicates that fewer Koreans considered immigration as an alternative pursuit for better options. That is, unlike in the late 1960s and the early 1970s when upper class Koreans tended to immigrate to the U.S., in the late 1980s the economic development brought an increased standard of living to Korea, which resulted in a tendency that people avoid the risks of emigration when they already enjoy prestigious positions in their own countries. Another contributing factor might be the knowledge of the living conditions of Korean immigrants in the United States, which include operating businesses in low strata neighborhoods, risking their lives, working from dawn to night, and lacking alternative opportunities.

The above speculation is convincing when the changes in the demographic characteristics of Korean immigrants are considered. Korean immigrants have been observed as a group to have high educational levels, white-collar, middle-class, and urban in origins (Light, 1980; I. Kim, 1981, 1987; Waldinger, 1989; Kim and Hurh, 1985; Min, 1988; Yoon, 1991c). According to my observations in the Atlanta Metropolitan Area, among Korean first-generation immigrant entrepreneurs who received educations in Korea, 53.2% of the interviewees had college or higher educations, whereas 46.8% of interviewees had high school, vocational school, or unfinished college education.

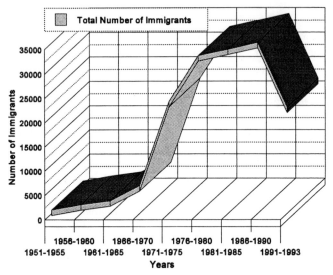

Figure 4-1: Changes in Flow of Korean Immigration

Sources: U.S. Department of Justice. Immigration and Naturalization Service.
Annual Reports: Immigration and Naturalization Service, 1966-1977; ibid.
Statistical Yearbook of the Immigration and Naturalization Service, 1979-
1993.

Although the absolute percentage of Korean immigrants in Atlanta
with high education is still higher than immigrants from other
countries, the Korean immigrants in Atlanta with high levels of
education are significantly fewer than in other large cities where over
80% of them have college educations (Yoon, 1991b). Considering that
a large portion of Korean immigrants in Atlanta came in the 1980s, it
can be suspected that the recent immigrants tend to have lower human
capital than their older cohorts. Thus, we can speculate that those who
have prestigious status in Korea are less attracted to immigration for
alternative, which results in the decrease of new arrivals from Korea.
Detailed comparisons of Korean immigrants on the basis of time of
immigration will be discussed in the Chapter V.

OCCUPATIONAL BACKGROUND OF KOREAN IMMIGRANTS AT ENTRY

Table 4-2 displays major occupations that Korean immigrants held before immigration. Figure 4-2 also shows a transitional tendency in occupational background of Korean immigrants at the time of entry. Managers and professionals include medical doctors and those held executive, administrative, and managerial jobs in Korea. Office workers represent sales and administrative support or clerical, and blue collar includes such workers as precision production, craft, repair, operator, fabricator, and laborer. Other occupation includes farming, forestry, fishing, and service.

A tendency is apparent in that the number of Korean immigrants with professional and managerial background drastically increased in the 1960s. The increase was caused by the influx of medical professionals, which reflects the influence of the Amendments of 1965 that emphasized admission of immigrants with specialized skills or occupations. Although there was some decrease, professionals and managers are the most dominant occupational backgrounds of Koreans who immigrated to the United States throughout the early 1970s. The proportion of all other occupations in the late 1960s and the early 1970s has low and marginal representation among Korean immigrants

In the late 1970s and 1980s, however, the proportion of professional and executive managers dropped to half of those professionals and managers immigrated in the late 1960s and the early 1970s. Although professionals and managers continuously have the highest representation of Korean immigrants, Koreans with occupational background other than professionals and managers became a significant portion of Korean immigrants from the late 1970s to the early 1980s and then declined continuously from the late 1980s to the early 1990s. The proportion of those with backgrounds such as office workers and other occupations were consistently low and insignificant, except that a drastic increase in the number of other occupations in the 1990s occurred because of an unusual large proportion (19.8%) of those with backgrounds in farming, forestry, or fishing were admitted in 1991.

Table 4-2: Major Occupations of Korean immigrants at the Time Admitted (%)

Years Admitted	Total	Managers & Professionals [1]	Office Workers [2]	Blue Collar [3]	Other Occupations [4]	No Occ. or not Reported [5]
1960	1,507	5.7	1.1	0.5	0.5	92.2
1965	2,165	5.1	1.6	0.6	0.7	92.0
1970	9,314	18.6	1.9	3.1	1.8	74.7
1975	28,362	14.0	3.7	7.0	2.5	72.8
1980	32,320	8.3	2.5	5.9	2.6	26.2
1985	35,253	7.9	3.6	3.4	2.5	82.6
1990	32,301	9.9	5.9	4.6	4.2	75.5
1993	18,026	13.4	3.8	3.1	3.0	76.8

Source: U.S. Department of Justice. Immigration and Naturalization Service. *Annual Reports: Immigration and Naturalization Service, 1966-1977*; ibid. *Statistical Yearbook of the Immigration and Naturalization Service, 1979-1993*.

[1] Includes Professional Specialty & Technical and Executive, Administrative, & Managerial
[2] Includes Sales and Administrative Support or Clerical
[3] Includes Precision Production, Craft & Repair and Operator, Fabricator, & Laborer
[4] Includes Farming, Forestry & Fishing, and Service
[5] Includes Housewives, children of immigrants and others with no occupations or not reported

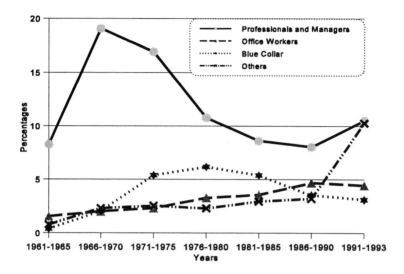

Figure 4-2: Trends in Occupational changes of Korean Immigrants

Sources: U.S. Department of Justice. Immigration and Naturalization Service.
   Annual Reports: Immigration and Naturalization Service, 1966-1977; ibid.
   Statistical Yearbook of the Immigration and Naturalization Service, 1979-
   1993.
* Professionals and Managers include Professional Specialty & Technical and
   Executive, Administrative & Managerial.
* Office Workers include Sales and Administrative Support or Clerical.
* Blue Collar includes Precision Production, Craft & Repair and Operative, and
   Operator Fabricator, & Laborer.
* Others include Farming, Forestry & Fishing, and Service

   The high proportion of Korean immigrants in the no occupation or
not reported category in the early 1960 is a reflection of the situation
that only Koreans in a particular condition could immigrate due to the
limitation put on Asians. For instance, most of the immigrants were
women married to American service men or war orphans adopted and
entered as immediate relatives of the U.S. citizens. In the 1970s and
1980s, on the other hand, although the immigration of U.S. soldiers'
wives and orphans continued, since the total number immigrants
increased drastically, the proportion of no occupation or not reported in

this period rather represents wives and children of legal immigrants of Korean households. Another condition in recent years, that caused a high proportion of Korean immigrants in the category, is that the immigrants would rather not report their occupations when they apply for immigration according to "family sponsored preference" because immigration on the basis of occupational and credential background is far more difficult than family sponsored immigrations.

BACKGROUNDS OF STATUS-ADJUSTED KOREANS

Table 4-3 and Figure 4-3 displays classes upon entry of the Korean immigrants who adjusted their status from temporary visitors or residents to permanent residents. Most consistently, visitors for pleasure and students are the two major components who have changed their status from temporary visitors to permanent residents. The visitors for pleasure are those who came with visas as tourists or for other purposes of visiting temporarily, and did not go back after their visa expired. Light and Bonacich (1988: 139) name them "visa abusers." The visitors for pleasure might have come to the U.S. for the initial purpose of becoming illegal immigrants, disguising their purpose as tourists. The proportion of visitors for pleasure became the major group who changed their status to permanent residents in the late 1980s.

The second major group is students. Until 1970, students constituted the major body who changed their status to permanent residents. And then, the proportion of this group fluctuated continuously at lower levels than in the early years. The fluctuation in the percentages of students seems to reflect social and economic situations in Korea at the time. In the earlier years, only members of the upper classes could afford the expense of studying abroad. In the case of students in the 1960s, once they came to the U.S., they might not have wanted to go back to Korea, one of the poorest countries in the world at the time.

In the early 1980s when the Korean government opened the door for studying and traveling abroad, and in the late 1980s when the Korean standard of living rose considerably, large numbers of Koreans started to pour out of Korea for better educational opportunities and for travel. In the late 1980s, a greater number of Korean students left Korea for studying abroad than any other period in Korean history, so there

Table 4-3: Class Upon Entry of Korean Immigrants Who Adjusted Status (%)

Years Admitted[1]	Total Adjusted	Visitors for Pleasure	Students[2]	Classes upon Business Related Visitors[3]	Entry Workers & Employees[4]	Others and Unknown[5]
1966	598	17.6	65.1	2.2	1.0	14.2
1970	2,079	29.5	52.3	6.8	1.5	9.9
1975	2,364	18.4	21.0	11.8	3.3	45.4
1979 [6]	2,602	30.0	17.4	16.7	1.5	34.4
1985	4,721	38.0	21.7	16.2	7.1	17.0
1990	6,335	25.4	17.6	5.1	7.6	44.2
1993	5,651	38.8	22.2	2.7	17.6	18.6

Sources: U.S. Department of Justice. Immigration and Naturalization Service. *Annual Reports: Immigration and Naturalization Service*, 1966-1977; ibid. *Statistical Yearbook of the Immigration and Naturalization Service*, 1979-1993.

[1] Data for Koreans as a separate category is not available for the years earlier than 1966.

[2] Includes Spouses and Children

[3] Includes Visitors for Business, and Treaty Traders and Investors

[4] Includes Temporary Workers, and Intracompany Transferees who are employed by an international firm or corporation with position of managerial executive or with special knowledge.

[5] Includes legalized Korean immigrants from 1989, whose status became legal permanent residents by IRCA

[6] Data for the year of 1980 and 1981 is not available

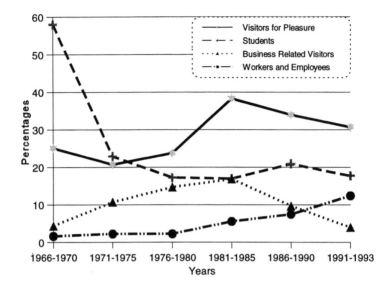

Figure 4-3: Classes of Korean Immigrants Who Adjusted Status

Sources: U.S. Department of Justice. Immigration and Naturalization Service.
Annual Reports: Immigration and Naturalization Service, 1966-1977; ibid.
Statistical Yearbook of the Immigration and Naturalization Service, 1979-
1993.

would have been a potentially larger number of Koreans who could
change their status. Among my interviewees, a pharmacist, two
businessmen, most lawyers, and all doctors came as students and
changed their statuses.

The third significant category is business related visitors, which
includes visitors for business or Treaty Traders and Investors. This
category is influenced by the U.S. Immigration law of 1976 that
permitted visitors to the U.S. to acquire permanent resident status, if
those visitors invested the minimum requirement of $40,000. In
acquiring permanent resident status, the Korean immigrants used the
legal system of investing capital in business enterprises such as wig
stores, liquor stores, garment shops, and so forth (I. Kim, 1981: 36).

Despite the fact that the rationale for acceptance of "investment
immigration" was to draw foreign capital into the U.S. to stimulate the
economy, this law has been utilized by immigrants to put efforts into

acquiring permanent resident status. Yoon (1993: 31) denotes that some wealthy Korean businessmen, high-ranking government officials, and professionals emigrated to the U.S. in the early years, bringing large amounts of money by utilizing their legal status as investors. In the mid-1980s, a significant proportion of Korean immigrants changed their temporary status to permanent resident for business related reasons.

A noticeable tendency is that in the 1990s, there is only a marginal number of Koreans who changed their status for business reasons. The provisions of the Immigration Act of 1990 raised the amount of capital required for investment immigration once again and provided a way for persons with "substantial trade" or "substantial investment" to change their status from temporary visitors to permanent residents. The Immigration and Naturalization Service defines "substantial trade and investment" as follows:

> An alien seeking treaty investor status must show that the investment is a substantial proportion of the total value of the business or the starting cost of the business in the United States, and that the investment is not the main source of living . . . The substantiality of an investment should be determined by the investor's ability to meet the "proportionality test" and the "marginality test", and not by a fixed dollar amount. . .The "proportionality" test is. . .the lower the value of the business enterprise, the higher the percentage of actual investment required. For a business investment with a total value of less than $500,000, the investor must have invested at least 75% of the total value of the business. For a business enterprise with a total value of less than $3,000,000 but more than $500,000, the investor must have invested at least 50% of the total value of the business. Similarly, an investor with a business enterprise which is valued at more than $3,000,000 is required to have minimally invested 30% of the total value. . . [If it is a marginal investment,] a business investment which offers employment opportunities for United States workers should also be given favorable consideration.[4]

On the one hand, the increased amount of required capital might be responsible for the sudden decrease of business related visitors in the 1990s. On the other hand, it is plausible to see the sharp decrease of investors or businessmen as a consequence of the economic development and increased living standards in Korea. Koreans who are able to invest as much as $500,000 would be hesitant to immigrate, because they are able to have a comfortable life in Korea.

With regard to temporary workers and employees, Table 4-3 shows an abrupt growth in the number of them hired at international firms in 1992 and 1993. In addition, the impact of the IRCA is shown in the category of others in 1989 through 1991. The number of the legalized Korean immigrants pushed the proportion in the category of others and unknown up after many years of decline.

GENERAL MECHANISMS OF KOREANS TO BECOME PERMANENT RESIDENTS

Table 4-4 displays the percentages of Korean immigrants divided on the basis of mechanisms utilized to be admitted. The main mechanisms by which Koreans gain permanent residency are based on the preference system, which was modified in the Amendments of 1965. A quota system based on preference categories was first introduced in the Immigration and Nationality Act of 1952 (INA) "by giving a quota preference to skilled aliens whose services are urgently needed in the United States and to relatives of U.S. citizens and aliens." [5] The quota system of the Amendments of 1965 established a seven-category preference system for relatives of U.S. citizens and permanent resident aliens (for the reunification of families) and for persons with special occupational skills, abilities, or training (needed in the United States).[6] The Amendments also established a rule of excluding immediate relatives such as spouses, children, and parents of U.S. citizens from numerical limitation. These amended elements ultimately contributed as principal mechanisms to the Korean immigrant influx for the last two decades.

The preference system has two elements: those "immigrants subject to numerical limitation" and those "immigrants exempt from numerical limitation." The preference system applies both for the new arrivals and the status adjusted immigration applicants. The general mechanisms, by which both new arrivals and the status adjusted are

Table 4-4: General Mechanisms of Korean Immigrants to Be Admitted (%)

Years[1] Admitted	Total Admitted	Immigrants subject to numerical limitations						Immigrants exempt from numerical limitations			
		Family Sponsored Preferences				Employment based Preferences		Parents of U.S. Citizen[8]	Spouses of U.S. Citizen	Children of U.S. Citizen	Others
		1st Pref.[2]	2nd Pref.[3]	4th Pref.[4]	5th Pref.[5]	3rd Pref.[6]	6th Pref.[7]				
1966	2,492	0.5	2.2	0.0	0.2	9.1	0.6	1.7	52.0	23.8	1.2
1970	9,314	0.2	8.8	0.4	14.2	5.0	7.4	1.9	29.4	13.0	1.0
1975	28,362	0.1	16.7	0.3	29.9	10.0	4.7	3.1	8.0	11.4	7.7
1980	32,320	0.1	18.9	0.5	39.1	2.3	0.6	10.2	13.7	10.2	3.7
1985	35,253	0.3	25.5	2.3	19.4	3.1	4.6	11.1	12.2	18.3	3.2
1990	32,301	0.4	17.4	2.3	27.7	3.6	6.3	9.7	12.7	10.2	10.0
1993	18,026	0.6	7.9	2.5	11.8	7.4	21.8	9.4	17.4	12.5	2.4

Source: U.S. Department of Justice. Immigration and Naturalization Service. *Annual Reports: Immigration and Naturalization Service*, 1966-1977; ibid. *Statistical Yearbook of the Immigration and Naturalization Service*, 1979-1993.

[1] Fiscal years end June from 1966 to 1975 and September from 1976 to 1993.

[2] Includes unmarried sons and daughters of U.S. citizens and their children

[3] Includes spouses and unmarried sons and daughters of permanent resident aliens

[4] Includes married sons and daughters of U.S. citizens and their spouses and children

[5] Includes brothers and sisters of U.S. citizens (at least 21 years of age) and their spouses and children

[6] Includes Priority Workers and Professionals with Advanced degrees. Also includes spouses and their children except for the fiscal year 1966.

[7] Includes Workers in short supply or skilled and unskilled without advanced degree. Also includes spouses and their children except for the fiscal year 1966

[8] Parents of U.S. citizens became a subject for exemption for numerical limitation from 1967. As a result, the number of parents of U.S. citizens is included in 2nd preferences in earlier years.

admitted as permanent residents, enable us to discern how the mechanisms influence the change of demographics and characteristics of Korean immigrants over the years.

As discussed earlier, Table 4-4 shows that the 3rd preference for professionals under the employment based preferences abruptly increased in the late 1960s as the Amendments of 1965 intended. Although the table does not show a tendency of increased number of professionals in the 1970s due to the large proportion of 2nd and 5th preferences, the sheer number of professionals consistently increased and reached a peak in 1974 and 1975. However, there is a sharp decrease of professionals in 1978 that would be a ramification of the Act of October in 1976[7], which sets a restriction on foreign medical school graduates both immigrant and non-immigrant coming to the United States for practice or training in the medical profession. Korean medical professionals were attracted by the centralized system of American medical institutions, which furnishes well-equipped hospitals and ultimately provides a good environment for research (I.Kim, 1981: 147-154).

The majority of medical professionals admitted were physicians, nurses, pharmacists, and dentists. Some of these were admitted from a third country such as Germany, because a large number of medical-service Koreans went to Germany initially then decided to immigrate to the U.S. instead of going back to Korea (I. Kim, 1981). Influenced by the regulation in 1990 that the application of the preference system favored employment-based preferences over any other categories, the percentage of professionals and skilled immigrants increased considerably in 1992.

With regard to family sponsored preferences, the second (spouses, unmarried sons, and daughters of residents aliens) and fifth (brothers and sisters of U.S. citizens) preferences are the primary mechanisms by which Koreans immigrants entered for more than two decades, and the mechanisms which induced chain migration in the long run: second Preferences became notable from 1973; fifth started as early as 1970. From the 1970s until 1990, the fifth preference appears to be one of the most consistently strong mechanisms for Koreans to be admitted. Although the family sponsored preferences were meant to serve the humane goal of reunifying immediate relatives, the law has been utilized by Korean immigrants in that they apply as immediate relatives instead of occupational preferences which is a far more difficult way to obtain immigration visas. Since the preference requires prospective immigrants to have siblings in the United States, the requirement gave chances for Koreans who did not have any occupational specialties, and yet had a sibling in the U.S.

As shown in Table 4-2, the lack of occupational specialty for those who immigrated under the fifth preference might have led to a high proportion of Korean immigrants with "no occupation or not reported" for their occupational background in the 1980s. In other words, the family sponsored mechanisms tend to induce those with lower human capital to immigrate to the United States. Although there were some fluctuations, the two categories were consistently feasible mechanisms for Korean immigrants to utilize the most over the two decades. The two categories represent "chain" migration that plays a very significant role for immigrants both before and after arrival to the United States.

With regard to immigrants exempt from numerical limitation, from 1966 to 1970, the proportion of spouses of U.S. citizens and children of U.S. citizens is significantly high. As noted earlier, the high proportion indicates that wives of American soldiers and war orphans continued to come to the U.S. The category, spouses of U.S. citizens, kept its position as one of the major mechanisms since 1976 after a short period of decrease. However, the steady immigration rate of spouses of U.S. citizens since 1976 should be interpreted as most are spouses of young Korean immigrants rather than wives of American servicemen. Just as earlier immigrants at the turn of the century, Koreans immigrants prefer to marry Koreans raised in Korea rather than Koreans raised in America with a different cultural system and values; Korean immigrants are even more against inter-racial marriages.

Parents of U.S. citizens also become one of the significant categories for immigration after 1980. Although the proportion of parents fluctuates from time to time, it was even pace until 1993 when it reached to the peak. Yoon (1991b) found that some parents immigrated to give chances to their adult children to immigrate under the fourth preference, "married sons and daughters of U.S. citizens," and that the parents then remigrated back to Korea after accomplishing their purpose. Since it is known that parents of Korean immigrants often become baby sitters when their sons and daughters go to work, and that it is harder for the relatively older people to get adjusted to the American way of life and society without a knowledge of English, the older people would rather have migrated back after finding out the hardship of adjusting to life in America.

As the data indicates, it is clear that chain migration is pervasive as a mechanism of Korean immigration. As Massey et al. (1987) argue, the existence of friend and family ties in the United States is a significant element for encouraging immigration. Light and Bonacich (1988) also argue that chain migration arises at places where a viable number of people have already settled and where newcomers can get support from their predecessors (p.153). They found that there is a close relationship between the size of Korean population in 1970 and the increase in the Korean population in the 1980 (Light and Bonacich, 1988: 143). The close relationship indicates that Korean immigrants, or any immigrants for that matter, tend to immigrate to destinations where they can get support from their kin or friends, because those with such support find it easier to get help on residential places as well as expansion of networks with other community members for business opportunities.

Without support from their predecessors, new arrivals may not be able to make it through life in America. Especially in the established ethnic economy, even new arrivals without knowledge of the American social systems or English skills can get jobs in the Korean ethnic economy. As Light and Bonacich (1988) point out, the concentration of the Korean population in Los Angeles is induced by chain migration. In addition, Koreans would not have become one of the most populous Asian communities in Los Angeles if there had not been an established ethnic economy.

SUMMARY

The influx of Korean immigrants beginning in the late 1960s has made them one of the predominant groups of Asian immigrants throughout the 1970s and 1980s. Despite the large numbers of Korean immigrants and the high representation of Koreans among all Asian immigrants in earlier years, the number of Korean immigrants dropped inordinately in the 1990s. Table 4-5 shows the trends of Koreans' representation in proportion to total Asian immigrants.

Two groups of Korean immigrants can be distinguished: new arrivals and status adjusted. The new arrivals are immigrants who came from Korea by applying for immigration visas to the American Embassy in Korea. The status adjusted are immigrants who entered the U.S. under different visa status and acquired permanent resident status

Table 4-5: Korean Immigrants' Representation among Asian Immigrants

Years Admitted	All Asians	Koreans (%)
1960	23,864	6.3
1965	19,778	10.9
1970	92,816	10.0
1975	132,469	21.4
1980	236,097	13.7
1985	264,691	13.3
1990	358,581	9.5
1993	358,042	5.0

Sources: U.S. Department of Justice. Immigration and Naturalization Service. *Annual Reports: Immigration and Naturalization Service*, 1966-1977; ibid. *Statistical Yearbook of the Immigration and Naturalization Service*, 1978-1993.

in the U.S. When the Korean immigrants become admitted as immigrants, regardless of whether they are new arrivals or status adjusted, they call fall under the category of immigrants subject from numeric limitation or those subject exempt for the numeric limitation.

The three most predominant mechanisms to be admitted as adults are family-sponsored mechanisms: sons and daughters of U.S. citizens; siblings of U.S. citizens; and parents of U.S. citizens. The mechanisms contribute to an establishment of chain migrations. The implication of chain migration might be that the more "family-sponsored preferences" become the main mechanism for Korean immigration, the less it is necessary for the immigrants to be qualified for occupational or credential skills. The tendency results in demographic changes among Korean immigrants in terms of occupational as well as educational backgrounds. That is, the composition of professionals and managers among Korean immigrants has decreased over the years, although it consistently keeps its proportion at a higher level than any other occupations.

On the other hand, the composition of blue collar or others has increased consistently in the 1980s until the recent years. That is, although massive Korean immigration started with professionals and people with special skills, once a mechanism of chain immigration is established, later immigrants seem less likely to be as qualified as their predecessors, because they instead utilized the "family-sponsored preferences," which do not require many individual skills or professions. However, in the 1990s there was an increase in the number of professionals and managers and a decrease in the number of Korean immigrants without occupations. In addition, Koreans tend to concentrate in a few particular regions such as California and New York. The concentration reflects occupational opportunities in those regions.

The established chain- migrations, the changes in demographics and occupational backgrounds, and the concentration of their residential regions in particular states are all important indicators how Korean immigrants enter into entrepreneurship or pursue to become entrepreneurs. Therefore, the following three chapters will explore how Korean immigrants in the Atlanta MA mobilize resources and become entrepreneurs.

NOTES

1. U.S. Department of Commerce. Bureau of the Census. *Population: General Report and Analysis* 1910-1960.

2. U.S. Immigration and Naturalization Service, *Statistical Yearbook of the Immigration and Naturalization Service*, 1993. Appendix 1.

3. U.S. Department of Justice. Immigration and Naturalization Service, *Annual Reports: Immigration and Naturalization Service*, 1966-1977; U.S. Department of Justice Immigration and Naturalization Service, *Statistical Yearbook of the Immigration and Naturalization Service*, 1978-1993.

4. 8 Code of Federal Regulations, Part 214. Customs Duties. The Office of the Federal Register National Archives and Records Administration. 1991. (56 FR 42952).

5. U.S. Department of Justice. Immigration and Naturalization Service, *Statistical Yearbook of the Immigration and Naturalization Service*, 1993. Appendix 1.

6. ibid.

7. ibid.

8. U.S. Department of Commerce. Bureau of the Census. *Census of Population and Housing, Supplementary Reports about Metropolitan Areas* Washington, D.C.: GPO 1990.

CHAPTER V

Pre-Immigration Background and Employment Experiences after Immigration

This chapter will discuss general background, employment experiences, and motivation for starting businesses of Korean immigrant entrepreneurs in the Atlanta Metropolitan Area (MA). Immigrants are naturally disadvantaged in the labor market due to a lack of political power and social status (Aldrich et al., 1984). In addition, antagonism against ethnic groups from the host society contributes to the exclusion of immigrants from occupations with prestige (Bonacich, 1972). Given the situation, immigrants will utilize every available resource to overcome their disadvantageous position in the society. Among useful resources, family networks were determined to be one of the most prominent resources that are utilized to get into the labor market and to start businesses (Werbner, 1987). Likewise, educational background is another acclaimed resource for getting jobs and establishing businesses (Chiswick, 1984; Light, 1984).

Therefore, the first question is whether or not Korean immigrants with family networks or higher levels of education have better job opportunities in the labor market or have better opportunities getting into entrepreneurship. The second question is what are the incentives for Korean immigrants to pursue entrepreneurship, rejecting employment opportunities in the labor market. By examining these issues, we can uncover how the concurrence between disadvantages in the labor market and advantages of personal resources encourages

Korean immigrants to pursue entrepreneurship more often than other job opportunities.

BACKGROUND OF KOREAN IMMIGRANT ENTREPRENEURS

Table 5-1 shows personal backgrounds on the basis of the time of immigration. Earlier immigrants are those who immigrated from 1965 to 1979. And later immigrants are those immigrated from 1980 to the 1994 when the interviews were conducted. With regard to educational background, the teenage migrants are separated out from the first generation immigrants because they mislead data. High proportion of the teenage immigrants have college education, of which attainment of college educations were in the U.S. and most of them came to the U.S. in 1970s. As a result, the teenage immigrants cause high proportion of those with college education among the earlier immigrants when they are categorized on the basis of time of immigration. However, since educational backgrounds of the first generation immigrants are important factor in the analysis later, the teenage immigrants are separated in educational background.

The pre-immigration networks refer to family networks that immigrants had family member who immigrated to the U.S. earlier and provided legal support for them to immigrate on the basis of family sponsored preferences. Again, the teenage immigrants are in a separate category because they immigrated with their parents when they were young and when they were not major decision makers for immigrations. Therefore, it is hard to include them in either of the categories, chain migrants and non-chain migrants.

As the table shows, the time of immigration is associated with human capital of Korean immigrants. The earlier Korean immigrants have higher proportion of those with college education than the later immigrants. Although the educational level of the later groups is still higher than that of immigrant groups from other countries, it is relatively lower than the earlier group. In addition, comparing to the earlier immigrants, almost two folds of the later immigrants came with pre-immigrant networks as chain-migrants. As shown in Table 4-4 in the Chapter IV, there was the drastic increase in chain migrants induced by Family Sponsored Preferences from the 1970s. As a result, the

Table 5-1: Background of the Korean Entrepreneurs (%)

	Earlier immigrants	Later immigrants	Total
Total number of interviewees (N)	56	103	159
Educational background			
College graduates	48.2	46.6	47.2
Non-college graduates	26.8	49.5	41.5
Teenage immigrants (college)	17.9	1.9	7.5
Teenage immigrants (non-college)	7.1	1.9	3.8
Possession of pre-immigrant networks			
Chain-migrants	23.2	55.3	44.0
Non-chain migrants	51.8	40.8	44.7
Teenage immigrants	25.0	3.9	11.3

number of brothers and sisters of U.S. citizens, parents of U.S. citizens, and unmarried sons and daughters of U.S. citizens increased to a large proportion of the total number of Korean immigrants each year.

Considering the two factors simultaneously, the factors have a mutual interaction influencing background of Korean immigrants, in that the earlier cohorts tended to have immigrated based on their own occupational and credential backgrounds, whereas the later immigrants tend to have relied upon family assisted immigration as chain-migrants. In other words, the increase in chain migration tend to influence the decrease of human capital of immigrants because the chain migration does not require for immigrants to show the individual credential and occupational background which is associated with educational background. The chain-migration further have an impact of a consistent decrease of Korean immigrants with professional and managerial backgrounds and the increase of blue collar immigrants from the mid-1970s to the mid-1980s.

Table 5-2 shows proportions of Korean immigrant entrepreneurs who have experiences of being employed after immigration and the types of occupations that they held before entering entrepreneurship. The employment experiences provide information about how Korean immigrants assimilate economically after immigration. In addition, the types of occupations reveal the status of Korean immigrants in the labor market, and how far they could reach in the ladder of an economic hierarchy. The table also shows Korean immigrants whose employment

**Table 5-2: Prior Employment Experiences of Korean
Entrepreneurs after Immigration**

	Earlier immigrants	Later immigrants	Total
Total number of interviewees (N)	56	103	159
Entrepreneurs with prior employment experiences (N)	44	87	131
Employment experiences at Korean-owned businesses (%)	27.3	110.3	82.4
Types of occupations of Koreans after immigration (%)[1]			
Cashiers[2]	9.1	58.6	46.6
Blue collar workers[3]	65.9	36.8	55.0
Other labor workers[4]	15.9	51.7	42.7
White collar workers[5]	13.6	10.3	13.7
Professionals[6]	9.1	3.5	6.1

[1] The percentages are on the basis of entrepreneurs with prior employment experiences. Since a large proportion of Korean immigrants had been employed in more than one type of job, the total percentage is over 100% of those with prior employment experiences.

[2] Cashiers include those who have worked at grocery or retail stores

[3] Blue collar workers include factory workers, postmen, mechanics or repairmen, construction workers, workers at dry cleaning stores.

[4] Other labor workers include janitors, waiters and waitresses, cooks, and hairdressers.

[5] White collar workers include secretaries, insurance or real estate agents, soldiers, newspaper companies, engineers, workers at bank, textile designers, librarians, and computer programmers.

[6] Professionals include doctors, lawyers, pharmacists, Asian medicine doctors, and accountants.

experiences are at Korean owned businesses, and whose employment experiences presumably have helped in establishing the current businesses.

As the table shows, most Korean immigrants tend to have employment experiences before entering into entrepreneurship. Korean immigrants have employment experience both in the mainstream labor market and in the ethnic economy where Korean small business owners hire coethnic labor. Among the types of occupations, blue collar workers, white collar workers, and professionals include types of employments in the mainstream labor market. On the other hand, cashiers and other blue collar workers are types of employments in Korean ethnic labor market. Regardless of time of immigration, Korean immigrants tend to find employment in marginal jobs in spite of their high educational or credential background in Korea. As the types of jobs indicate, Korean immigrants seem to struggle with underemployment by working in low-paid and low-skilled occupations with little promise of economic mobility.

A noticeable tendency is that a great proportion of the earlier immigrants have employment experiences in the mainstream labor market at blue collar jobs, whereas a significantly high proportion of the later immigrants have been employed at businesses owned by Korean entrepreneurs relying upon the coethnic community for employment opportunities. Despite that the earlier immigrants have high credential qualifications when they entered the United States as immigrants, a large portion of them seem to have been stranded in jobs with little privileges, such as manufacturing work on assembly lines, steel work at construction companies, chemical companies, electronic manufacturers, or janitorial work at maintenance companies. Only immigrants in the 1960s with medical credentials had employment experiences in the white collar jobs as doctors or medical trainees.

Considering the types of employment, prior employment experiences, in general, are perceived to be negative in the sense that they had limited opportunities for promotion and in getting privileged occupations. A college-graduate non-chain migrant entrepreneur who had worked as a mechanical designer said,

> Although I had pursued a white collar occupation, I did not have a chance because my license acquired in Korea was not recognized in the labor market and my language skill was not sufficient at the level required in the job market. In addition, although it was my turn to be promoted in my section, an American who was less experienced than me got a promotion. I thought it was because I was an immigrant and a minority.

The earlier immigrants came to the U.S. and established Korean communities on their own, whereas the later immigrants have come to the U.S. to fit into already established Korean communities. As a result, differences in the structure of the Korean communities lead the later immigrants to experience different employment opportunities and the ways of adjusting to the new society. In the 1980s, Korean communities across America were well established, particularly in large cities where the number of Korean businesses drastically increased. Due to the situation that job opportunities in the coethnic community increased, later immigrants have the inclination to heavily rely on the coethnic labor market.

Those employed in the coethnic labor market tend to have worked as laborers at small businesses owned by Korean immigrants. Their employment experiences in the coethnic labor market presumably are more marginal than those of the mainstream due to lower wages and a lack of security. In the coethnic labor market, they acquire such jobs as cashiers at grocery stores, truck drivers, janitors, waiters, waitresses, welders, or dish washers. As a result of the large number of later immigrants with employment experiences in the coethnic community, types of employment have shifted from blue collar occupations in the mainstream labor market to laborer's jobs at Korean-owned small businesses. Thus, the types of employment are more homogenized regardless of their educational background or possession of family networks.

Despite the marginal characteristics of employment at Korean businesses, they have advantages in the coethnic labor market in that they provide job opportunities for newcomers, that allow them to learn business skills from working at the businesses, which enhances the possibilities of starting their own businesses in the future. As interviewees note, employment experiences in the coethnic labor market seem to have clear benefits for those starting their own businesses. An interviewee who immigrated in the late 1980s said,

> I learned skills and information relevant to business operation as I was working at a Korean business. To operate my own business, it was necessary for me to find out where I can buy those products and which product are suitable to the customers whom I target. Since I operate a business for black customers, I shelve products that black customers prefer. You will find differences in merchandise that I sell here from the merchandise sold at Krogers where whites are the majority of customers.

Therefore, an ethnic labor market in the Korean community is to be utilized by most members of the community regardless of their personal background such as educational background and possession of family networks.

The increased proportion of those employed in the coethnic labor market among the later immigrants is suggestive of three phenomena among Korean immigrants in the 1980s: (1) as the Korean entrepreneurial communities in the United States enlarged, induced by the increased number of Korean immigrants over the period, more job opportunities would have been created in the coethnic labor market by the increased number of Korean businesses; (2) Koreans who immigrated since the 1980s came with a great deal of knowledge about Korean-owned businesses in the U.S., and thereby might have initially started working at Korean-owned businesses to learn skills for business management, intending to operate their own businesses in the future. The initial intention to become entrepreneurs at the time of immigration might have an influence on the shorter periods taken for later immigrants to establish businesses; (3) the less selective characteristics of Korean immigrants might have caused them to encounter higher barriers in finding even blue collar jobs in the mainstream labor market and forced them to rely more on the coethnic community for job opportunities.

The first and second phenomena are vividly shown in a comment by a chain-migrant with employment experience at his sibling's business:

> I was employed by Koreans. The business was owned by my sister. I have not thought of getting a job outside nor did I intend to be employed for a long period of time. I opened my business not very long after immigration because I knew I could make more money by running a business. I collected information from my friend whom I got close to after immigration. And I started this business as a partnership with a friend of mine.

Bonacich (1973) considers immigrant entrepreneurs "middleman minorities," who are "oppressors" by exploiting immigrant laborers at minimum wages. This is true to the extent that immigrant entrepreneurs pay low wages to the coethnic laborers. However, some immigrants are willing to work for such low level of wages for the purpose of learning skills rather than making money or providing business capital. Immigrant entrepreneurs and coethnic laborers encounter an unfamiliar and often hostile economic environment in the host society. As a result, both entrepreneurs and workers establish an ethnic economy (Light, 1994) and mutually help each other to overcome unfavorable situations. For instance, workers provide the labor force and entrepreneurs furnish business information and skills.

Therefore, the ethnic labor market plays two roles: one is to have the immigrant laborers as cheap source of labor that gives coethnic immigrant entrepreneurs a competitive advantage; the other is to provide job opportunities for newcomers as well as to provide a place where potential entrepreneurs learn information or skills for their own future businesses.

FAMILY NETWORKS AND EDUCATIONAL BACKGROUND

In response to a disadvantageous structural and social environment in the labor market, immigrants mobilize all possible resources for job or business opportunities. One of the prominent resources is family networks (Sanders and Nee, 1996). As shown for pre-immigration networks in Table 5-1, family networks are sources that chain-immigrants have before immigration which enable them to acquire information about their destination. Family networks are fundamental resources that spread and thereby minimize risks involved in long distance migration, that enhance personal security and mental comfort, and that contribute to the establishment of social relationships at the destination (Tilly, 1990). Taylor (1986) argues that, more importantly, migration networks are crucial for immigrants' occupational pursuits and their adjustment to the new society. Consequently, chain-migrants have better economic prospects of employment or career opportunities in the destination due to available information acquired through networks (White, 1970). Therefore, family-kinship networks for immigrants are imperatives for economic and social survival in their destination venues (Lomnitz, 1977).

Migration networks enhance economic opportunities in the destination countries because the connections help to increase income by providing job information (Tilly, 1990), and by generating capital and information for entrepreneurial pursuits (Goldberg, 1985). The utilization of family networks enables some immigrants such as Koreans to stand out in entrepreneurship (Light et al., 1993). Therefore, immigrants with family networks would be expected to be in a preferable position for better jobs in the labor market as well as for more opportunities for entrepreneurship.

Chiswick (1984), on the other hand, argues that educational attainment and occupational background in the country of origin are the crucial factors for immigrants' job opportunities after immigration. Therefore, immigrants with higher levels of education and greater occupational experience have more advantageous earning opportunities in the destination (Bates, 1997; Chiswick, 1979, 1984; Light, 1984; North and Houstoun 1976). As a result, Korean immigrants with class resources and/or family network ties are expected to have better prospects for economic assimilation than those without.

I. Kim (1987) found in New York that a Korean aphorism in the immigrant community states that operating a business is the fastest way to get ahead in America. Indeed, Korean immigrants devote much of their time to pursuing entrepreneurship after immigration. If it is a general consensus that immigrants can economically get ahead only through entrepreneurship and that entrepreneurship is the fastest way of getting ahead, it would be reasonable to believe that most Korean immigrants are eager to be entrepreneurs. Therefore, more successful immigrants in terms of economic achievement are those who start a business immediately after immigration or who establish one in a shorter period than other members in the community.

Table 5-3 examines this assumption by investigating prior employment experiences of interviewees based on educational level and possession of family networks (chain-migrants). The table is divided on the basis of two factors—possession of family networks and educational background—since family networks and educational backgrounds have been perceived as the most prominent resources that influence employment and entrepreneurial prospect of immigrants.

Teenage migrants are separated because most of them have employment experiences and have been employed for a long period, which will result in a distortion of data. Since the teenage migrants acquire an education in the U.S., they tend to have pursued employment in the mainstream labor market as average Americans would. Given their situation, they tend to have been employed much longer than their first generation immigrant parents before starting their businesses. However, as it will be discussed in the later section of this chapter, they also found limits and disadvantages due partially to their position of being a minority, and partially to some of them having limited language skills. Since their experiences tend to mislead the general tendencies of employment experiences of immigrants, they are analyzed separately.

Table 5-3: Prior Employment Experience(s) of Korean Entrepreneurs

	Chain migrants	Non-chain migrants	Teenage migrants	Total
Total number of interviewees (N)	70	71	18	159
Those with no prior employment(s) (%)	20.0	18.3	5.6	17.6
Those with prior employment(s) (%)	80.0	81.7	94.4	82.4
Average duration of prior employment(s) (yrs.)	2.8 2.3 *	3.2 3.0 *	4.4 4.0 *	
Employment experiences at Korean businesses (%)	96.4	81.0	41.2	82.4

	College graduates	Non-college graduates	Teenage migrants	Total
Total number of interviewees (N)	75	66	18	159
Those with no prior employment(s) (%)	26.7	7.6	5.6	17.6
Those with prior employment(s) (%)	73.3	89.4	94.4	82.4
Average duration of prior employment(s) (yrs.)	2.2 2.0 *	4.0 3.3 *	4.4 4.0 *	
Employment experiences at Korean businesses (%)	76.4	100.0	41.2	82.4

*Medians

"Those with no prior employment" are the entrepreneurs who started their businesses immediately after immigration. On the basis of this variable, we can speculate who has the most favorable circumstances to start a business without struggling in marginal occupations. "Those with prior employment," on the other hand, are the entrepreneurs who have been employed before becoming entrepreneurs. "Average duration of prior employment" is mean number of years that the interviewees have been employed before starting entrepreneurship. On the basis of these two variables—those with prior employment and duration of prior employment—we can speculate how quickly Korean immigrants establish their businesses after being employed. "Employed at Korean-owned businesses" is the percentage of the entrepreneurs who have been employed by Korean small business owners before starting an entrepreneurship. This variable indicates the frequency that Korean immigrants rely upon their coethnic community for employment opportunities.

With regard to those with no prior employment, the table shows a great discrepancy in the proportion who started their businesses without employment experiences on the basis of educational background rather than possession of family networks. The clear tendency is that a higher proportion of college-graduates have started businesses without suffering in low-paid and low-skilled employment in the labor market. On the other hand, there is no considerable difference in the percentages of those starting businesses immediately after immigration on the basis of possession of family networks. The tendency indicates that educational background is considerably important to establish businesses immediately after immigration. Although class resources are argued as determining resources for the success of ethnic entrepreneurship (Light, 1984, 1985; DiMaggio, 1982), the argument neglects to acknowledge how higher levels of education are useful not only for the management of businesses, but also for the establishment of entrepreneurship. However, as shown in the table, class resources are one of the decisive indicators for entering entrepreneurship without struggling through a period of underemployment.

An interviewee with a college education who immigrated in the early 1970s explains his absence of employment experience as follows:

> I did not even think about getting any kind of job because I had friends whom I knew since our university-days and who were willing to help me start a business. I collected business information from my friend before immigrating. And, as I observed other Korean entrepreneurs making a tremendous amount of money that I had never thought about in Korea, I was more eager to start a business than to get any other type of job. In addition, my friend told me that my college degree would not have been very helpful to gain any kinds of white collar jobs, but left me in blue-collar jobs with frustration induced by barriers and disabilities. Even in blue-collar jobs, there would have been a limit in promotion. The situation, therefore, had compelled and encouraged me to venture into entrepreneurship rather than white collar jobs. I also became less interested in white-collar jobs because of incomparably lower earnings compared to entrepreneurship at the time.

The interview indicates that school-based friend relationships were decisive for starting his business at the beginning. Therefore, social networks on the basis of friend relationships and of educational background seem to have played a decisive role in the decision to enter entrepreneurship.

The duration of prior employments shows that, again, educational background is a crucial resource, in that those with higher levels of education take less time to enter entrepreneurship than those with other resources. On the other hand, family networks are also beneficial resources, in that those with family networks take less time for establishing businesses than those without family networks. Therefore, in accordance with the predictions of network theory, chain-migrants seem to have advantages in establishing businesses in shorter period. However, class resources as determined by educational background have a stronger influence than family networks, in that college-graduates establish their businesses more quickly after immigration than those with or without other resources such as family networks. The only non-college graduates who started their own businesses in a shorter period were those who immigrated with specific skills that have demand in the Korean community such as hair dressing or auto repair.

Periods taken for business establishments become more consistent when interviewees are divided on the basis of the time of immigration. Among the earlier immigrants, the impact of educational background consistently provides advantageous situations to enter entrepreneurship in a shorter period after being employed. College-graduates also seem to be much more successful in business establishment without suffering in the labor market than non-college graduates. Counter to predictions of network theory, among the earlier immigrants, those with family networks took rather longer to establish businesses, thereby chain-migration does not seem to be advantageous for business establishments in shorter periods after being employed. Therefore, class resources seem to have a considerable impact on whether or not Korean immigrants need to be employed for capital or other resource mobilization before starting businesses, and how shortly after the immigration they can establish their own businesses.

Class resources of the later immigrants are not a strong predictor of an immediate start in businesses after immigration. Nonetheless, the class resources are consistently influential in determining how quickly businesses are started after being employed. A difference in tendencies among the later immigrants is that chain-migrants establish their businesses in a shorter period than non-chain migrants. However, when the two factors, class resources and family networks, are compared simultaneously, it is the case that those with higher educational backgrounds are more successful in starting businesses in a shorter period than those with family networks.

What the data suggest, therefore, is that a higher level of education consistently has an impact on the economic success of immigrants. By the same token, family networks do not seem to promise economic success as consistently as educational level does. However, when data is divided on the basis of family networks and educational level simultaneously, family networks are beneficial for business establishment only when immigrants have a higher level of education. Therefore, although family networks are expected to be advantageous for economic achievement after immigration for establishing entrepreneurship (Massey et al., 1987), educational background and the time of immigration, both of which reflect class resources, are more influential for economic achievement in the new country.

Regarding those who have been employed at Korean-owned businesses, Table 5-3 indicates a greater number of those with lower educational background and the chain migrants tend to rely on the ethnic economy in the Korean community. However, non-chain migrants also rely heavily on the ethnic economy by a small difference in the proportions. On the contrary, few of those with higher educational background rely on the ethnic economy for employment. That is to say, regardless of the possession of family networks or educational background, newcomers tend to significantly rely on coethnic business owners for employment opportunities.

In addition, as shown in Table 5-3, there is a big discrepancy in the percentages of those working for coethnic employers on the basis of educational level. As Table 5-2 displays, however, a vast majority of the later immigrants were more dependent upon the job opportunities in the Korean community than were their earlier cohorts. The reason that a lower proportion of college graduates are reliant on the ethnic labor market is that a high proportion of college graduates are the earlier immigrants who tend to have had employment experiences in the main stream labor market rather than in the ethnic labor market. Therefore, the discrepancy is due to the earlier immigrants who came to the U.S. when the Korean entrepreneurial community was yet to be established.

According to the assumption of network theory, chain-migrants are expected to have more access to job opportunities at those businesses that they access through connections with family networks. However, the frequency of prior employments for chain-migrants does not show a more eminent tendency over non-chain migrants. Instead, regardless of family networks, the majority of Korean immigrants tend to be underemployed in the marginal sector. Therefore, job opportunities in the coethnic labor market are favorable to all the coethnic members in the community (Portes and Manning, 1986) and Korean immigrants tend too look for job opportunities in the coethnic labor market (Wilson and Portes, 1980).

In general, teenage migrants tend to have been employed in the mainstream labor market and the duration of employment is generally longer than that for the first generation immigrants. As indicated earlier, the types of jobs that teen migrants held include both white collar and blue collar jobs, and vary from lawyer to auto mechanic according to their educational background. This indicates that although teen migrants might have had opportunities to find occupations in the mainstream labor market, they seem to be discouraged in the labor market and eventually look for an alternative in entrepreneurship.

Teenage migrants seem to get into the mainstream spontaneously, if they have a higher educational background. However, there is a tendency that teenage migrants with higher educational backgrounds have a longer employment experience in the mainstream labor market than those with lower educational backgrounds. For instance, college-graduates tend to have worked as white collar workers such as engineers or lawyers, whereas non-college graduates tend to have worked as blue collar workers such as auto mechanics. A high proportion of the teenage migrants were able to get white collar jobs, since they have been brought up in America, and naturally pursue careers in the mainstream labor market.

However, in most cases, they do not seem to be successful in getting prestigious jobs even when they have a high educational background. One of the reasons might be insufficient language skills, since some of them immigrated in their late teens and did not develop language skills sufficient to get prestigious jobs. Also, there might have been a discrimination factor. For example, one interviewee who immigrated when he was 11 years old and became a lawyer experienced discrimination in the mainstream labor market which constrained his opportunity for promotion and compelled him to pursue his own legal practice in the coethnic economy.

Table 5-4 displays types of prior employment of Korean immigrant entrepreneurs separately on the basis of available resources—family networks and educational background. This table illustrates how class resources or family networks are related to getting prestigious jobs. The teenage immigrants are included in chain migrants since they immigrated according to their parents' immigration status. "Blue collar workers," "white collar works," and "professionals" include those with employment experiences in the mainstream labor market, whereas "other labor workers" and "cashiers" include those with employment experiences in the Korean ethnic economy. The relatively higher proportion of white collar workers among chain migrants and college graduates is due to the teenage migrants with college educations from America who worked at white collar occupations.

Excluding the teenage immigrants, however, neither the educational background nor family networks seem to provide opportunities to get prestigious jobs in the mainstream labor market or the ethnic economy where Korean immigrants operate businesses. Chain-migration does not seem to furnish Korean immigrants with better occupational opportunities, in that the only jobs available for Korean immigrants seem to be marginal jobs with low-wages and requiring low-skills both in the mainstream and the ethnic labor market. In general, regardless of their educational background, Korean immigrants seem to be underemployed without success at getting jobs with prestige or security in the labor market.

As network theory argues, immigrants with family networks have advantages for job opportunities by relying on the coethnic community. However, chain-migration does not promise job opportunities with prestige. For instance, regardless of possession of family networks, most Korean immigrants have worked at marginal jobs such as janitors in the mainstream and cashiers in the Korean-owned businesses. As displayed in the earlier tables, although class resources do not seem to confer better job opportunities in the mainstream labor market, they clearly have on advantageous impact on business establishment.

Therefore, family networks are not such a powerful economic asset for immigrants to get prestigious jobs or pursue entrepreneurship. Instead, human capital has a much greater impact on immigrants' economic achievement after immigration. Family networks, however, seem to be slightly beneficial only when they are accompanied by a higher level of education. The tenency that class resources are a more

Table 5-4: Types of Prior Employments of Korean Entrepreneurs after Immigration (%)

	Chain migrants	Non-chain migrants	Total
Total number of interviewees (N)	88	71	159
Those with employment experiences (N)	73	58	131
Types of occupations of Koreans after immigration [1] (%)			
Cashiers [2]	42.5	51.7	46.6
Blue collar workers [3]	49.3	62.1	55.0
Other labor workers [4]	43.8	41.4	42.7
White collar workers [5]	20.5	5.2	13.7
Professionals [6]	5.5	6.9	6.1
	College graduates	Non-college graduates	Total
Total number of interviewees (N)	87	72	159
Those with employment experiences (N)	66	65	131
Types of occupations of Koreans after immigration [1] (%)			
Cashiers [2]	50.9	45.8	46.6
Blue collar workers [3]	43.6	62.7	55.0
Other labor workers [4]	36.4	54.2	42.7
White collar workers [5]	14.5	11.9	59.5
Professionals [6]	10.9	1.7	6.1

[1] The percentages are on the basis of entrepreneurs with prior employment experiences. Since a large proportion of Korean immigrants had been employed in more than one type of job, the total percentage is over 100% of those with prior employment experiences.

[2] Cashiers include those who have worked at grocery or retail stores

[3] Blue collar workers include factory workers, postmen, mechanics or repairmen, construction workers, workers at dry cleaning stores.

[4] Other labor workers include janitors, waiters and waitresses, cooks, and hairdressers.

[5] White collar workers include secretaries, insurance or real estate agents, soldiers, newspaper companies, engineers, workers at bank, textile designers, librarians, and computer programmers.

[6] Professionals include doctors, lawyers, pharmacists, Asian medicine doctors, and accountants.

prominent resource for establishing immigrant entrepreneurship rather than family networks will be discussed further in the Chapter VI in relation to social networks as a resource.

MOTIVATIONS TO START BUSINESSES

A question arises concerning the propensity that Korean immigrants are inclined to start their own businesses instead of pursuing jobs in the mainstream labor market. What causes Korean immigrants to move away from job opportunities in the mainstream labor market to establish businesses?

Despite the help obtained from family networks at the destination, immigrants are disadvantaged in the labor market due to lack of information, insufficient and/or untransferable skills, and exclusion from the mainstream. As a result, immigrants are compelled to seek occupations in less desirable labor markets where working conditions are harsh and wages are low (Waldinger, 1989; Bonacich, 1973). Therefore, their motivations to pursue entrepreneurship may be reflected by their previous labor market experiences.

It is commonly known that Asian immigrants, including Koreans, are more likely to move up the socio-economic ladder than other immigrants (Light, 1984; Rose, 1985; Waldinger et al. 1985). However, as shown in the earlier section, the jobs available for Korean immigrants tend to be marginal. Therefore, the employment available for them in the labor market of the new society does not provide security or future. In addition, the labor market situation is unfavorable for them, in that they encounter competition with natives and that they are more disadvantaged due to non-transferrable job skills or insufficient language skills.

Consequently, instead of getting jobs in the mainstream labor market immigrants are more likely to pursue entrepreneurship in the new land than they might have been if they had stayed in their country of origin (Shapero and Sokol, 1982). Although business ownership may not be considered a great leap of social mobility, it promises better economic conditions than wage employment in the labor market (Aldrich et al., 1984). Thus, it is reasonable to speculate that a large proportion of immigrants uses entrepreneurship as a means of upward mobility because of disadvantages and barriers in the labor market (Light, 1972, 1984; Portes and Back 1985; Wilson and Martin, 1982). As a result, although entrepreneurship requires hard work, the marginality of employment in the labor market combined with the promise of better economic prospects in entrepreneurship are strong motivations to start businesses. Therefore, it is necessary to examine how the limited opportunities are perceived by Korean immigrants who become entrepreneurs.

Table 5-5 shows the motivations that inspired Korean immigrants to turn to entrepreneurship. Since respondents have multiple reasons becoming entrepreneurs, each group has over 100% for the total percentage of motivations. The factors are not mutually exclusive, in that "poor language skills," "lack of information," "untransferable skills or low educational level," and "labor market disadvantage and limit" bind them into marginal occupations with "low wages in jobs available." In addition, since the only jobs available are marginal occupations with low wages, small business operations promise "better economic prospects" as well as "independence" from the labor market where immigrants encounter limitations and barriers.

The major motivations to turn to entrepreneurship, in general, are better economic expectations and insufficient language skills. They all seem to have struggled with their insufficient language skills in the labor market, which induces disadvantages such as limited promotional opportunity. However, there is a subtle difference in the consideration of English skills and economic mobility as motivations on the basis of their educational background. Those with higher human capital were motivated to start businesses more passionately in order to gain economic achievement, thus avoiding limited opportunities as immigrants in the mainstream labor market. Although those with a higher educational background also suffered disadvantages in the labor market as much as those with a lower educational background, a more import factor for them to start businesses was a confidence that they will attain economic achievement in entrepreneurship. Consequently, the limited opportunities caused by poor English skills are a rather minor reason for them to pursue entrepreneurship. Instead, economic mobility is a greater attraction.

For instance, those with a higher educational background, especially those who immigrated in the 1970s, deliberately gave up employment opportunities because the opportunities were limited, on the one hand, and because entrepreneurship provided incomparably higher economic returns, on the other hand. A college-graduate who immigrated in the late 1970s shows enthusiasm for getting into entrepreneurship when he says,

Table 5-5: Motivations for Becoming Entrepreneurs (%)

	College graduates	Non-college graduates	Total
Total number of interviewees (N)	87	72	159
Better economic expectations	43.7	37.5	41.5
Poor language skills	24.1	55.6	38.4
Lack of information	3.5	6.9	5.0
Untransferable skills or low educational level	8.1	19.4	13.2
Labor market disadvantage and limit	26.4	26.4	26.4
Independence	29.9	9.7	20.8
Low wage in jobs available	8.1	15.3	11.3

> Business is the quickest way of making money. Because it is impossible to get a white collar job with my poor language skills, I have never thought about applying for one. I wanted to be independent instead of being told what to do. And I also knew I could make a lot of money by running businesses. We had very good business by catering to black customers when I first immigrated. The business was just booming then. Businesses catering to black customers took a downturn when the U.S. government cut a large portion of welfare for poor people. It directly affected the consuming behavior of black customers. That was one of the reasons why my previous business failed, and I moved to Atlanta searching for business opportunities.

As a consequence, the implications of independence are a disassociation from the limited opportunities and marginal employment in the labor market and a confidence for starting their own businesses. As the table shows, therefore, the percentage of respondents who refer to "independence" as a motivation to enter entrepreneurship is considerably higher among the college graduates compared to the non-college graduates.

Contrary to those with higher human capital, those with lower human capital were motivated rather by frustration in that they found that there were no opportunities for them to pursue better economic status in employment. As the table shows in the category "low wage in jobs available", those with lower human capital joined entrepreneurship to move out of "extreme poverty" rather than to attain economic achievement. Getting into entrepreneurship for those with lower educational background is considered to be a reaction to the labor market situation; insufficient language skills give them disadvantages and limits in the labor market; and the deficiency constrains them in only occupations that they can hardly sustain their living after immigration. The poorer language skills of non-college graduates compared to those of college graduates ultimately induces an initial exclusion or more limited opportunities in the labor market. Although they also expect better economic prospects in entrepreneurship, frustration for the poverty level living standard is a more fundamental reason to turn to entrepreneurship.

An entrepreneur with lower educational background expresses that the motivation to start businesses is a reaction to a marginal level of wages induced by poor language skills. An interviewee who immigrated in the late 1980s and suffered in a marginal job said,

> Prospects in the job market were worse than I imagined in Korea. There is just no choice in the job market. Janitorial work does not provide enough even for a minimum level of living. I did not immigrate just to be a janitor, but I had some prospects in better living after immigration. So, I pursued entrepreneurship because there was business information available in the Korean community.

In addition, among those who immigrated in the 1980s, some college-graduates also experienced a stiff limitation in opportunities caused by insufficient language skills. As a result, some of the later immigrants with college educational backgrounds, who endured hardship at marginal jobs in the labor market, chose business entrepreneurship as an alternative. Therefore, the college graduates among the later immigrants were motivated by the same reasons as those with lower educational background such as the language barrier, which left low-wage jobs as their only alternative.

A large number of respondents who immigrated in the 1980s, regardless of educational level, said that extremely "low wages" were the motivation to become entrepreneurs. For example, a college-graduate who immigrated in the late 1980s, and who had been employed at marginal jobs in the labor market and chose to operate his own business instead said,

As an immigrant, there was no choice other than running my own business. I had no way of getting a white collar job as I did in Korea because I cannot speak the language fluently. The jobs available just do not provide enough for living. Also, the prospect in employment was unclear, because promotion is limited for immigrants. Given these situations, business was a better way of making a living and was a way to make more money than employment in the mainstream labor market.

Limited opportunities for immigrants, non-transferable skills, and insufficient English language skills seem to coincide to create a situation in which Korean immigrants are disadvantaged in the labor market and are compelled to search for an alternative occupational opportunity, which is entrepreneurship. One interviewee considered entrepreneurship as the only desirable alternative to labor market employment and said,

Most jobs available were physically demanding and low-wage. I thought an operation in a business to be an alternative. Although a business operation equally demands physical effort, economic returns in businesses are better than employment and a business operation pays back as much as I work.

Korean immigrants are excluded not only due to insufficient language skills, but also due to subtle discrimination. A lawyer, who immigrated at the age of eleven and does not have a problem with English, said,

I have been employed at a law firm run by a white person before and worked for four years. My dilemma there was that the firm always sent me minority customers such as Vietnamese, Hispanics, or Chinese. Because of the situation, my opportunities were limited. If I were going to have only minority customers, it was not necessary for me to be employed by them because I have a better chance on my own. So, I made a decision to open my own office near Korea Town, where I can serve a great variety of minorities such as Koreans, Vietnamese, Hispanics, and Chinese.

Although in general, running one's own business is considered to be an alternative to lower-status employment, it does not seem to be a great economic leap for some entrepreneurs. A non-college graduate interviewee does not feel satisfied by his business operation and shows frustration with limited opportunities both in business and jobs. As he said,

> I would rather get a job working at an office, if there is anything available. But there simply are no available jobs, partially because I do not have such a high educational background, and partially because I am an immigrant who does not know much about society and who cannot speak the language fluently. Businesses in Korea town do not provide enough to make a living because the number of customers is limited. And if I am employed by someone, I would make as little money as I do now, but I would have less stress.

Therefore, Korean entrepreneurs are motivated to pursue business ownership because of the coexistence of an advantage in the ethnic economy and a disadvantage in the labor market. The disadvantage is that immigrants are disproportionately concentrated in lower level occupations because labor prices are predetermined for immigrants before their entry into the labor market (Bonacich, 1973; Light, 1979; Piore, 1979; Sassen-Koob, 1980). On the other hand, the advantage is that immigrants have internal solidarity in the immigrant community that excludes competition with outsiders of the community (Light, 1980). Thus, ethnic economies established by coethnic members not only provide job opportunities for new immigrants, but also facilitate them with skills and resources for their own future businesses. As Aldrich et al. (1984) argue, immigrant entrepreneurship is to some extent a negative adaptation to the unfavorable opportunity structure of the receiving society. Subtle discrimination, furthermore, becomes more significant for those with higher human capital. On the other hand, those with lower human capital or insufficient language skills are precluded from the initial stage of entry into jobs in the labor market, which promises prestige or future.

SUMMARY

Although networks are conceived as a device to supply essential information (i.e., the setting up of businesses, the economic inputs required, the problems likely to be encountered, and labor requirements), chain-migration for Koreans does not seem to make them utterly advantaged in their economic pursuits after immigration. That is, family networks do not seem to provide an advantageous situation for business establishment or prestigious jobs.

Instead, class resources such as educational level have a distinctive impact on economic pursuit in the U.S. through entrepreneurship. Although higher class resources do not promise better employment opportunities in the mainstream labor market, the data clearly suggest that higher class resources provide advantages enabling Korean immigrants to establish businesses in a shorter period or to bypass harsh employment experiences in the labor market.

As a result, the network argument does not support the situation of Korean chain migrants in Atlanta. Then, the questions are whether or not networks are altogether unnecessary for immigrants' economic pursuits, and what aspect of class resources provides such an advantageous position for entrepreneurial pursuit. The answer is that networks are still one of the most crucial elements for immigrants in adjusting to the new society.

However, what network theorists in general have overlooked are the distinctions among various types of networks and the way in which different networks operate to generate different resources necessary for immigrants' economic pursuits. Therefore, networks should be contemplated on the basis of who the members are in the circle of networks and how the networks are established by different groups of people. These elements make some networks distinctive from others. Therefore, the next chapter discusses what resources are utilized for business establishments, and how and what kinds of networks have been established to generate such resources.

CHAPTER VI

Networks and Resource Mobilization

As shown in Chapter V, class resources available on the basis of educational backgrounds are crucial for entering entrepreneurship. As a result, the issues to be examined here are what aspect of class resources plays such a crucial role for immigrants' economic achievement, and how the educational backgrounds of Korean immigrants has been transformed into resources for business establishment. Although researchers (Bates, 1994a, 1994b, 1997; Sanders and Nee, 1996) argue that class resources become essential for entrepreneurship, it is not clear how educational background transforms into resources. Therefore, this chapter examines how educational background is capitalized by Korean immigrants. Since higher educational background itself is a vague resource that cannot be evaluated on its own for its usefulness as an instrument for starting businesses, educational background will be examined in relation to social network establishment and resources generated from these social networks.

FAMILY NETWORKS AND SOCIAL NETWORKS

As demonstrated in the previous chapter, Korean immigrants enter entrepreneurship because of limited opportunities in the labor market and/or insufficient language and non-transferable technical skills. In addition, in contrast to what some have predicted, family networks of Korean immigrants do not seem to provide more advantageous means to pursue business establishment. That is, despite the expectation of network theory that chain-migrants are in a more advantageous position for economic pursuits such as entrepreneurship (Goldberg, 1985; Light et al., 1993; Lomnitz, 1977; Taylor, 1986; Werbner, 1987), they do not show an advantageous status in pursuit of business establishment. Instead, it was shown that higher educational background appears to be more influential for business establishments (i.e., starting businesses either immediately after immigration or shortly after being employed).

Therefore, questions arise concerning the pervasive assertion that networks are an advantageous resource for immigrants' economic pursuits, and what aspect of class resources provides such an advantageous resource for entrepreneurial pursuit. The point is that networks are a very important resource for immigrants' economic pursuit in conjunction with educational background. However, what theorists in general have overlooked are the distinctions between family networks and social networks and the ways in which social networks are interconnected with educational background. Therefore, this study will show how social networks are established and utilized to become one of the most crucial elements of immigrants' economic pursuits in the new society. In addition, as Rubinson and Browne (1994) argue that educational background contributes to economic mobility when it is combined with an appropriate social situation, this study will also show how educational background is closely related to network establishment and influences resource mobilization.

As pervasively accepted, networks are fundamental resources that immigrants utilize for their economic pursuits. However, it is important to note that family networks and social networks function and operate separately and generate different resources. Despite the two distinctive components of networks, most network theorists tend to contemplate the two components of networks—family networks and social networks—in one concept of network ties (Werbner, 1987, 1990; Zimmer and Aldrich, 1987). Some examine only one or the other side of networks (Aldrich and Zimmer, 1986; Boyd, 1989). Others treat social networks as ethnic resources in the community (Goldscheider and Kobrin, 1980). In addition, although the researchers acknowledge the critical importance of social networks in the community for business information (Werbner, 1987), they often neglect to examine the differences in utilization of social networks from family networks and the process of social network establishment in conjunction with educational background.

However, social networks are established and operated differently in the community from family networks. Therefore, networks should be divided into two separate types: namely, family networks and social networks. This division will allow us to examine how social networks are established and become crucial to generate resources for business establishment and how they operate differently from family networks for resource mobilization. Family networks are based on connections with family or relatives which Korean immigrants already had in America before immigration. Thus they facilitate a legal status for immigration as "family sponsored preferences." Those who immigrate based on their family networks are known as chain migrants. Social networks, on the other hand, are based on connections with members in the community other than family or relatives, which Korean immigrants establish after immigration by entering the ethnic community, and which often reflect the immigrants' human capital and socio-economic background in the country of origin.

Korean immigrants enter the community in several ways: (1) chain-migrants are introduced by their family members; (2) some enter through involvement in organizations; (3) some enter by working at coethnic businesses. Therefore, it is reasonable to predict that those with some kinds of ties such as family or friends enter the community easily and establish trust more quickly than those without the trust which will ultimately become useful for resource mobilization to enter entrepreneurship. The data in this chapter are divided only on the basis of educational background since we found in Chapter V that family networks do not provide a more advantageous situation for business establishment.

CURRENT BUSINESSES

Table 6-1 shows general characteristics of current businesses. Retail and wholesale trades are the most common types of businesses that Korean immigrants in Atlanta operate. Retailers cater to two economic niches: one in the enclave for Korean customers; and the other in the non-enclave for non-Korean customers, the majority of whom are inner city African Americans. The majority of wholesalers, on the other hand, cater to Korean customers as well as customers from a variety of other ethnic groups who own retail stores in the inner city neighborhoods. On the basis of this connection, Korean retailers and wholesalers have mutual benefits, in that retailers get benefits for credit and business information, and that wholesalers have a steady supply of customers (Yoon, 1991a).

Table 6-1: Current Businesses (%)

	College graduates	Non-college graduates	Total
Total number of interviewees (N)	87	72	159
Types of current business(es)			
Professionals[1]	14.9	1.4	8.8
Wholesale and retail trade [2]	40.2	51.4	45.3
Restaurants [3]	11.5	5.6	8.8
Service [4]	19.5	4.2	12.6
Personal service [5]	4.6	18.1	10.7
Other service [6]	9.2	19.4	13.8
Own multiple businesses	20.7	29.2	24.5
Number of employees in the current business(es)			
No employees	20.7	30.6	25.2
1 or 2 employees	34.5	34.7	34.6
3 to 5 employees	21.8	15.3	18.9
More than 6 employees	23.0	19.4	21.4
Annual gross sales			
Under $30,000	2.3	5.6	3.8
$30,000-$49,999	9.2	11.1	10.1
$50,000-$99,999	14.9	18.1	16.4
$100,000-$299,999	26.4	27.8	27.0
$300,000-$499,999	23.0	13.9	18.9
$500,000-$999,999	4.6	11.1	7.5
$1,000,000 or more	14.9	9.7	12.6

[1] Professionals include doctors, accountants, lawyers, pharmacists, and Asian-medical doctors.

[2] Wholesale and retail trades includes wholesales, Korean food grocery, gift shops for Korean goods, health food store, furniture stores, book stores, clothing stores, general merchandise, beauty supply, jewelry and accessory stores, liquor store, grocery, convenient store, flower shop, and drapery shop.

[3] Restaurants include Korean food restaurants and fast food restaurants.

[4] Service includes real estate and insurance agents, community newspapers or broadcasting station in Korean, travel agencies, and various institutions for teaching dancing, math, English, computer, and martial art.

[5] Personal service includes car mechanics, repair stores (i.e., computer, electronics, jewelry, shoe, and cash register), alteration, and beauty solon for Korean customers.

[6]Other service includes video rental shop, photo studio, print and sign shop, billiard store, moving company, construction company, coin laundry and dry cleaning, and building cleaning company.

In addition, such types of business as professionals and service reflect the educational backgrounds of entrepreneurs. Professionals are a reflection of their majors in college such as law, medicine, Asian medicine, or accounting. However, there is one professional who is a non-college graduate and became an Asian medical doctor on the basis of his prior employment experience at a Asian medical practice in Korea. Service businesses such as real estate and insurance agents also seems to be operated mostly by college graduates due to their relatively better English language skills or due to a shortage of capital to start such businesses with better economic affluence. Service businesses such as institutes also operated mostly by college graduates, reflect their majors in colleges in Korea for teaching various subjects. On the other hand, most personal service and other service businesses tend to be operated by non-college graduates because they require mechanic or repair skills.

The number of employees and annual gross sales illustrate size and economic performance of businesses. The table indicates that a majority of Korean businesses are small with either no employees or a couple of employees. Despite that a slightly higher proportion of non-college graduates have multiple businesses, it is college graduates who have a higher proportion with larger businesses and more employees. In addition, annual gross sales demonstrate that a slightly higher proportion of college graduates tend to have businesses with better economic returns than their counter part.

In sum, a considerably large proportion of Korean entrepreneurs in Atlanta are concentrated in small businesses whose types are selling merchandise. Educational background tends to divide the characteristics of businesses, in that it influences the types of businesses entrepreneurs start and college graduates tend to have slightly larger businesses with better economic performance.

SOCIAL NETWORK ESTABLISHMENT

This section focuses on how social networks are established after immigration. This analysis investigates how the established networks influence the capacity to mobilize resources. Social networks are different from family networks in that friends or acquaintances become constituents of the networks rather than parents, siblings, and relatives. The social networks tend to be established on the basis of human capital brought from Korea. Therefore, the examination of social network establishment in conjunction with educational background shows the characteristics of the networks, and thereby unveil the way in which resources are generated by social networks. In addition, it helps determine the causes of the discrepancy in business establishment on the basis of educational level shown in Chapter V.

Korean immigrants tend to create a variety of organizations in the Korean communities (I. Kim, 1981). Werbner (1990: Ch. 10) argues that activities centered around organizations and associations revive not only ritual and religious practices, but also produce internal political and financial resources. The political and financial resources mobilized through the community relationships enable immigrants to compete successfully in the economic, professional, and political arenas. Therefore, the following section will examine patterns of organizations and associations in the Korean community, for the organizations and associations become a foundation of social networks with other members, and also are considered to be beneficial for immigrants' economic pursuits.

Table 6-2 shows the numbers of associations and organizations in the Korean community in Atlanta as of September 1995. Considering the number of Korean immigrants in Atlanta, approximately 40,000 measured by the Korean community organization, Korean immigrants have a large number of associations and organizations. Among the organizations and associations, churches are the most numerous, followed by university, and high school and middle school alumni associations.

Table 6-3 presents the number of associations with which each interviewee is involved on the basis of educational level. The table allows us to examine how Korean immigrants are actively involved in associations largely for the purpose of developing social networks. As Table 6-3 shows, college-graduates tend to be more active participants

Table 6-2: Number of Associations and Organizations in Atlanta

Types of organizations & associations	Numbers
Korean governmental offices	2
Korean business associations	13
Interest groups (political & professional)	15
Hobby clubs	13
University alumni	27
Churches	97
Non-profit organizations	13
Cultural associations	6
Student organizations	5
Religious organizations	11
High and middle school alumni	27
Buddhist temples	3
Total	232

Source: East-South Weekly, 1995 September
(A Korean Newspaper published in the Korean community in Atlanta)

Table 6-3: Number of Associations Involved (%)

	College graduates	Non-college graduates	Total
Total number of interviewees (N)	87	72	159
None	10.3	23.6	16.4
One	47.1	52.8	49.7
Two	21.3	13.9	18.2
Three or more	20.7	9.7	15.7

in associations and organizations in that they are more likely to be involved with multiple associations and organizations. In particular, the earlier immigrants with college educations are the most active participants in associations, typically being involved in more than two associations and playing a significant role in the Korean community in Atlanta. Therefore, college-graduates seem to establish social networks far more actively than non-college graduates through the associations and organizations.

On the other hand, non-college graduates are relatively less active, in that a large proportion of them are involved in a single association, and a lower proportion of them are involved in multiple associations. In addition, a higher proportion of non-college graduates have no involvement in any community organizations, revealing their reluctance or indifference to be involved with these types of organizations. Those who cited involvement in only one association tend to be exclusively involved in churches more than any other associations. As a result, a large proportion of non-college graduates tend either to involve in church or in no association. Considering the general notion that networks are crucial for resource mobilization, the active involvements in associations or organizations help them acquire more business resources. In addition, resources generated through social networks tend to insure occupancy in better economic niches, which will be discussed in the Chapter VII.

PATTERNS OF ASSOCIATION INVOLVEMENT

Table 6-4 displays the types of organizations and associations in which interviewees are involved within the Korean community in Atlanta. Patterns of involvement in these associations allow us to speculate the way in which Korean immigrants in Atlanta establish social networks in the community. As shown in Table 6-3, some are involved in multiple associations, whereas some are in a single association or none. "Korean church" is considered as one of the associations because it generates resources necessary for the economic activities of Korean immigrants. Teenage migrants are separated, since they show no difference in association involvement on the basis of educational background, which results in a distortion of the tendency of network establishments in the ethnic community.

Table 6-4: Types of Association Involvement of Korean Immigrants' (%)

	College graduates	Non-college graduates	Teenage migrants	Total*
Total number of interviewees (N)	75	66	18	159
Korean churches	61.3	60.6	61.1	61.0
Alumni associations	42.7	4.5	0.0	16.4
Community associations	12.0	12.1	11.1	11.9
Business associations	22.7	18.1	22.2	20.8
Hobby clubs	6.7	6.1	11.1	6.9
None	12.0	21.1	16.7	16.4

*Since a large proportion of Korean immigrants are involved in more than multiple associations, the total percentage is over 100%.

Churches

As Table 6-2 displays, the most numerous associations are churches and school alumni groups. There is a fairly large number of Korean churches, when considered in terms of the population of Korean immigrants in Atlanta. In addition, considering that about 61% of the interviewees responded that they attend church regularly, Korean church seems to be the most common place to meet other community members due to the large number of Koreans involved in churches.

However, what makes church membership important is not only the large number of participants, but also the resources generated though church. The proportion of participants indicates that churches are the most open place to the community members for social network establishment after immigration. Furthermore, a large portion of business-related resources are generated at church, such as obtaining business information. Therefore, Korean immigrants are in an advantageous position to obtain the business information as a result of involvement in churches. Churches in the Korean community seem to be not only places for religious ceremony, but also for carrying out secular business by establishing connections among individuals in the coethnic community.

Many interviewees found their business sites through their church membership: i.e., some bought directly from their fellow church members and some learned information about businesses to be sold from fellow church members. The following interviewee seems to have taken a great advantage for a business establishment by being a church member:

> I was interested in this business because of the good and safe location. While one of my church members was running this one at the time, I consistently reminded her that, whenever she intended to sell this business, she should sell it to me. One day, she told me that she had an intention to sell this business and I immediately bought the business from her. I had wanted this business so much because the business is located in a large apartment complex where there is no problem of security and where sales volume does not fluctuate. Also, it is easy to run a business here because I was already familiar with this business by visiting my friend when she was running this business. The business hours were also a consideration in that I do not have to work from dawn to night like in grocery businesses.

More importantly, a large proportion of Korean immigrants have had employment experiences at Korean-owned businesses established by church members and acquired skills for business operation at those businesses. Some entrepreneurs obtained skills required for running businesses from fellow Koreans with whom they became acquainted at churches after immigration. The employment is not particularly related to making money, but rather to gaining information and skills for their future businesses. As an interviewee mentions,

> One of my church members was in this type of business. Since I heard that the economic performance in this type of business is steady, I asked this church member for further information about the business. I worked at his store for a while to learn skills and information related to this type of business. I worked until I became confident enough to operate one of my own.

Considering the high percentage of people involved in churches, churches seem to be the most prominent places for social network establishment. Since churches furnish members with business information and resources, it is known that a large portion of Korean immigrants, who were not Christians in Korea, start attending church after immigration. Especially for those who do not have any family connections, churches become a primary source for resource mobilization by enabling them to get to know people and to get involved in the community.

Interviewees were extremely reluctant to reveal the connection between their business interests and their church attendance. Some denied a relevance of attending church to their business operations. Despite their remarks or hesitancy to admit business interests in church, it has become a well-known "secret" that churches are one of the most common and open grounds for potential businessmen or for those intending to change business types in order to have an access to information. Since trust in the community is important for gaining further resources such as capital, labor, or information, the social relationships in church help to create the personal trust that ultimately facilitates business resource mobilization.

In addition, another advantage of church membership is finding new customers, especially for those with businesses in the enclave economy (e.g., Korean restaurants, real estate, insurance, and travel agencies, and auto body shops). One of the enclave business owners made the following remark:

> I go to church to meet people and make friends. I also join some hobby clubs for the same purpose. I can avoid loneliness on foreign soil by meeting Korean friends. Furthermore, I cannot separate church and business. I can pray for my business to God at church. At the same time, meeting friends ultimately benefits my business later, because all my friends become customers for my business.

Another interviewee also made a similar remark by saying,

> I not only obtain mental contentment as well as social gatherings at church, but also obtain information about business. I also want to have a positive influence for my children by attending church.

As interviews reveal, one of the major purposes for Korean entrepreneurs' going to churches is to "keep contact," which ultimately becomes a resource for their businesses by providing information and experience, or by finding customers for the businesses. In addition to business-related interests, so many Korean immigrants are Christians because church communities provide an environment of "a pseudo extended-family" (I. Kim, 1981: 199). In addition, "through church-centered activities Korean immigrants attempt to cope with their overwhelming sense of alienation from the larger society" (ibid).

Most interviewees in Atlanta who go to church reported a search for mental comfort as a reason for going to church rather than faith. In fact, very few refer to faith in Christianity as a purpose of going to church. In spite of the high proportion of church participants, only a few interviewees identified themselves as "believers" in Christianity and some said they started to go to church after immigration in order to meet people and, like the interviewee above, to avoid isolation in a foreign country. For example, one interviewee explained,

> Most people whom I met after immigration are church members. And my activities are very much related to events that occur in church. I meet Koreans and make friends at church. It is easy to become close friends at church because we share a lot of things in common such as faith, food, culture, or Korean songs. Most of all, I go to church to have some mental comfort after a week of making a living in the harsh outside environment.

Therefore, church seems to be a place where Korean immigrants establish social networks, where they mobilize business resources, and where they meet people to avoid a feeling of isolation by participating in cultural affairs.

Alumni Associations

The most distinctive tendency concerning the type of association involvement is displayed by the percentages of involvement with alumni associations. Although the total number of those involved in alumni associations is smaller than that for church members, the proportion of those involved in alumni associations significantly differs based on educational level. As Table 6-2 shows, there is an equal number of university alumni and high- and middle-school alumni. The number of both university and high- and middle-school alumni associations is the second most numerous after churches. However, a much larger proportion of college graduates are involved in alumni associations than non-college graduates.

Alumni associations provide social networks with different characteristics from those of churches. The alumni associations are based on the schools from which Korean immigrants graduated in

Korea, thereby revealing their socio-economic background. The importance in the tendency is that considering the strong solidarity among university alumni in Korea, the solidarity may well be extended to America. In Korean community newspapers, one the of the most frequently advertised announcements concerns regular meetings of various university alumni associations. As a result, those with college educational backgrounds have a stronger foundation for social network establishment. Through the strong solidarity, college graduates have an advantageous situation to develop trust and relationships in a relatively shorter period, which eventually provides resources for business establishment.

As Massey et al. (1987) note, a common origin from the native country creates a strong communal identity among immigrants in the United States. The shared identity not only produces and promotes cohesion of migrants, but also facilitates the pursuit of common goals. Church-related social networks in the Korean community can be established relatively randomly among members and can be shared by a rather larger population, whereas networks associated with alumni associations tend to be characterized on the basis of human capital acquired from Korea. Therefore, these alumni-based networks might provide resources that divide Korean immigrants into their respective paths of business establishments.

An interviewee mentioned the following about benefits for participation in alumni associations:

> I started my business after spending one year at a language program at a university located in New York. Since I once owned companies in Korea, I intended without a doubt to operate my own business after immigration. I also brought enough money to start a business, for I immigrated as an investment immigrant. While I was in New York, one of the senior alumni members from my university introduced me to another senior graduate, who works in a distribution office of a large kitchen furniture company in Korea. The senior in the distribution office was taking the responsibility of distribution in America. So, I import kitchen furniture from Korea through him and install it for newly constructed apartment complexes by contracting with American constructors.

As the interviewee mentioned, college graduates utilize alumni associations as another source to establish social networks, which, in many cases, are fundamental for business establishment. As a result, a higher educational background provides more ways of establishing social networks, and enables the immigrants to be active in the establishment of social networks. In turn, the active involvement and variety of social networks indicate more access to the resources necessary for business establishment.

University alumni associations strengthen their solidarity by holding meetings regularly. The university alumni associations therefore become a place where newcomers are introduced to old members and where social network connections in America are started. Once they are introduced and accepted through alumni associations, newcomers immediately acquire trust among the members in the associations. Also, if the alumni association is related to the elite universities in Korea, the members would gain a respected status in the community by participating in the community associations. As a consequence, the selectivity of membership might induce a situation in which only alumni members get access to business information and strategy, or gain trust for their further economic and social pursuits. On the other hand, all these forms of ready information would not be available for those who do not have a college education and who cannot become members of alumni associations.

An interviewee mentioned the business information available by participating in alumni associations when he said,

> When we have a regular alumni meeting, we first talk about agendas, how to ensure solidarity and run the association efficiently. But it does not take a long time for everyone to start talking about each others businesses. We talk about which businesses are doing well, which ones are not, or what kinds of businesses are better than the others. This is how I get information about businesses and get updated on better businesses.

In addition, although the table does not show it, educational level not only influences the establishment of social networks in alumni associations, but also all other associations and organizations in the community. For instance, among those involved in churches, relationships tend to develop along the line of educational background, and business information also tends to be circulated on the basis of background. Therefore, educational background is closely related social network establishment, which in turn influences resource mobilization.

As interviews reveal, the extensive trust and bonds established through alumni associations are beneficial only for those with higher levels of education and exclude non-college graduates.

Other Associations

While church and alumni associations are the most useful organizations for the establishment of social networks and resource mobilization, the Korean Association is the largest non-profit organization in the community. The Korean Association, like church membership, is open to everyone in the community, and benefits not only the members, but also everyone in the community. The association is, therefore, an organization that is ready to help Korean immigrants in need. However, while the association is a non-profit voluntary organization that helps newcomers with housing or jobs, they do not have a strong effect on resource generation for business establishment. Therefore, they are excluded from the analysis in this chapter.

However, to further investigate the Korean community association regardless of importance in resource generation, college graduates without family networks are relatively more active in this non-profit organization in the community. The majority of members involved with the Korean Association are earlier immigrants who came in the 1960s and early 1970s, whereas non-college graduates involved in the Korean Association immigrated since the 1980s. The leaders of the Korean association tend to be those with high educational background.

I. Kim (1981) examined the Korean community in New York and found that most professionals or businessmen, regardless of how successful they are in their areas, tend to take responsibilities for leading community lives. He argues that the tendency occurs not only because they are more qualified in terms of their knowledge of American society or economic status, but also because economic success or status acquired through their occupations do not "guarantee successful businessmen and professionals a commensurate status recognition in the larger society" (Kim, 1981: 204). That is, the leadership role assumed by professionals and businessmen in community organizations and churches is not only due to higher status based on human capital and economic background, but also due to the alienation that they experience from society at large.

With regard to business associations, entrepreneurs become members of business associations after entering particular types of businesses. Since business associations do not have a direct influence on resource mobilization to start businesses, they are not included in this analysis. However, to examine a general tendency of involvement in business associations, again a higher proportion of participants is college graduates, most of whom are also non-chain migrants. That is, as was found for the community associations, college-graduates are also the most active in the business associations and become more involved in the larger economy by participating in American business or professional associations. Those who participated in American business or professional associations tend to have immigrated in the 1960s and early 1970s. Although entrepreneurs become members of business associations after entering various types of businesses, the participation in business associations increases the possibilities of establishment for the social networks in order for Korean entrepreneurs to update business information and strategies from their peers even after becoming entrepreneurs.

In sum, college-graduates are more active in participating in associations or organizations in the Korean community, which furnish them with sources for social network establishment. In particular, the earlier immigrants with college education tend to be involved in a larger variety of associations. Consequently, those actively involved in associations and organizations have better chances for starting and maintaining social networks, which will provide useful information or business capital in the future. On the other hand, in general, there is no significant difference in the degree of involvement in associations or organizations according to the possession of family networks.

Teenage Migrants

Regardless of educational background, in general, teenage migrants are the most actively involved in church. However, in contrast to the first generation immigrants, teenage migrants tend to attend churches more for the religious purposes than for business interests. On the other hand, since alumni associations are a cultural phenomenon imported from Korea, teenage migrants who acquired their education in the U.S. do not form or participate in alumni associations. Naturally, they cannot participate in the existing university alumni associations because they do not have a connection with those Korean universities. However, the teenage migrants, most of whom a college graduates, actively participate in business associations.

RESOURCE MOBILIZATION AND NETWORKS

A prominent characteristic of networks is a function for resource mobilization necessary for business establishment. Based on social networks established in the community, Korean immigrants vigorously mobilize resources to establish businesses. As shown in the earlier section, networks are indispensable for information and capital mobilization for business establishment and operation. Korean immigrants rely heavily on information gained through network connections, mainly by word of mouth. In addition, "long term trust" and "personal reputation" provide capital through credit, personal loans, or RCA (Light et al., 1990; Werbner, 1990). The following two subsections examine how networks are utilized to generate such resources as information and capital.

Information Mobilization

Table 6-5 shows the sources of information mobilization to start businesses. Interviewees were asked how they collected information to start the current types and sites for their businesses. Generally, one of the most crucial resources for immigrants to become entrepreneurs would be information for business types and sites. Regardless of their educational background, Korean entrepreneurs heavily rely on social networks for information sources. As shown earlier in this chapter, social networks are established through involvement in church, associations, or organizations. In addition, employment experiences are another form of social networks, in that entrepreneurs established social networks as they were employed by Korean business owners in the ethnic economy either catering Korean customers or non-Korean customers. Therefore, social networks established through employment experiences at Korean businesses is another important source of information mobilization.

Furthermore, although the table does not show it, there is no difference in the source of information mobilization regardless of immigrants' possession of family networks. That is, it is social networks that they rely heavily on for business information regardless of their background. As a result, social networks established through involvements in organizations or through employment experiences are the fundamental source of business information available for members.

Table 6-5: Sources of Information Mobilization for Business(es) Establishment (%)

	College graduates	Non-college graduates	Total*
Total number of interviewees (N)	87	72	159
Social networks	34.5	38.9	36.5
Family networks	10.3	13.9	11.9
Employment experiences in the U.S.	21.8	41.7	30.8
Skills from Korea	9.2	16.7	12.6
Prior business experiences	10.3	12.5	11.3
Professional background **	14.9	0.0	8.2

*Since a large proportion of Korean immigrants utilized multiple sources of
  information mobilization, the total percentage is over 100%.
**Professional background includes lawyers, doctors, pharmacists, Asian
  doctors, and accountants.

Therefore, regardless of educational background or possession of family networks, social networks have a determining influence on business information mobilization for a majority of Korean entrepreneurs. An interviewee notes the importance of social networks as follows;

> After I immigrated, I made a friend who owns a jewelry store. He told me a jewelry store for black customers is a good business because store hours are shorter, it is physically less demanding, and most of all the business is safely guarded. So, I worked at my friend's shop for several months to learn how to operate this type of business. It was not for making money. I helped him for free because he was doing me a favor by teaching me where to buy merchandise and which kinds of items are popular. He even helped me to find a business site.

Reliance on employment experiences at Korean business for information mobilization is more significant for non-college graduates than college graduates. That is, non-college graduates more heavily rely on employment experiences after immigration, in that they utilize social networks for information mobilization in conjunction with employment experiences in the United States. In other words, non-college graduates tend to establish social networks as they live in a community for a long time and are employed at Korean-owned businesses, hence accumulate their personal trust from the community members. As a result, a high proportion of non-college graduates mobilize business information through a combination of social networks and prior employment experiences, and thus it takes them a longer period to establish social networks.

In particular, the most common source for non-college graduates without family networks to mobilize business information is prior employment experiences, partially because they do not have such organizations as alumni associations that provide prompt trust, and partially because they do not have family networks that introduce them to the community. Therefore, Koreans who immigrated with neither higher educational background nor family networks build up trust in the community on their own. Considering that non-college graduates heavily rely on prior employment experiences in the U.S., and that they develop social networks as result of previous employments, the consequence is that it takes longer for non-college graduates to establish social networks, which influences the longer time taken to establish their own businesses. This propensity provides partial evidence for the tendency that was discussed in Chapter V, in which non-college graduates tend to take longer to start their own businesses, whereas college graduates are more successful in establishing businesses in shorter period or without suffering from underemployment.

A non-college graduate who utilized his prior employment experience effectively for his own business establishment said,

> I worked at a Korean-owned grocery for about five to six years. During the employment period there, I accumulated experience on how to run businesses, especially a grocery business. It was very helpful to establish my own business because I could get access to information about business sites and because I learned skills to start my own business.

Non-college graduates have another distinctive characteristic in that some of them depend on skills that they developed in Korea such as hair dressing, electronic repair, or auto mechanic. Those with such skills tend to establish businesses in a shorter period, since they already have useful knowledge and skills to establish businesses. As a result, such skills seem to be important for those without family networks or a high educational. An interviewee skilled at hair dressing at the time of immigration seems to have utilized this skill for an employment opportunity as well as a business establishment, and said,

> I was not hesitant to start a hair salon after immigration, because I had a skill in this area. But I waited for a while, working at a Korean owned hair salon, because I did not know where to buy equipment or how this type of business is run differently from the way it is done in Korea. While I was working as a hair dresser, I made a friend who designed interiors and another friend who helped me buy equipment. When I got all the information needed to start a business, I quitted the job and opened my own hair salon.

Social networks established through employment experiences in the U.S. or skills developed in Korea are important sources for information, especially for non-college graduates who immigrated in the 1980s. For instance, 75.9% of non-college graduates who immigrated in the 1980s are dependent on their employment experience or skills for their business establishment, whereas only 30.4% of college graduates who immigrated in the 1980s are dependent on prior employment experience. Another way, not listed in the table that immigrant entrepreneurs use to collect information, is to survey the markets themselves. Two interviewees who collected information themselves gave examples as follows;

> I collected information myself by visiting business sites. I particularly looked at customer traffic and the composition of neighbors. I wanted to open a business in a neighborhood with a rather higher income for quality customers because the income level would definitely affect the level of sales volume.

> I looked up Korean newspapers published in Chicago. There was an article regarding good businesses for Korean immigrants to operate. In the article, they talked about grocery businesses. So, I particularly looked around for grocery businesses to open one for myself.

Excluding "professional background" which is not a normal method of information mobilization, the sum of the percentages of information sources is 86.1% for college graduates, whereas it is 123.7% for non-college graduates. The big discrepancy in percentage explains that those with a higher educational background tend to utilize a single source to mobilize information, whereas those with a lower educational background tend to utilize multiple sources. The tendency reveals that college graduates have one dedicated source for information, and thus do not put effort as much as their counterparts who seem to require more effort and time for information collection. Considering the tendencies that non-college graduates establish social networks while they are employed and collect information from multiple sources, the propensity again explains the tendency discussed in Chapter V that non-college graduates take a longer time to start their own businesses.

In sum, although there is a difference in the establishment of social networks either through friendship or prior employment experiences, the data demonstrate social networks are fundamental for information mobilization. Therefore, entrepreneurs are facilitated by social networks of continuing social relations that provide information and resources. On the other hand, despite that family networks have long been expected to be an important resource for business establishments, social networks seem to be far more pervasive sources for business information for Korean entrepreneurs, whereas family networks seem to have a minor influence for information mobilization.

Capital Mobilization

Table 6-6 shows sources for capital mobilization for business establishment. The sources of capital mobilization include personal savings, personal loans from various sources (i.e., friends, family, or relatives), bank loans, money brought from Korea, and RCA. Family networks indicate personal loans from family or relatives and social networks from friends. Money from Korea consist of the capital that Korean immigrants brought from Korea at the time of immigration to the United States.

The most widely used methods of capital mobilization for both the current and prior businesses are immigrants' personal savings and personal loans through family networks and social networks. The category, little capital required, is not mutually exclusive with the category, personal savings, because such businesses as private medical offices, insurance agencies, real estate agencies, travel agencies, or small size businesses have smaller capital requirements and, as a result,

Table 6-6: Sources of Capital Mobilization for Korean Immigrant Business(es)

	College graduates	Non-college graduates	Total *
Total number of interviewees (N)	87	72	159
Sources of capital mobilization for the current business (%)			
Personal Savings	67.8	76.4	71.7
Social networks	11.5	20.8	15.7
Family networks	23.0	38.9	30.2
Bank loans	26.4	20.8	23.9
Money from Korea	21.8	16.7	19.5
RCA (Kye)	5.7	11.1	8.2
Little or no capital required	13.8	2.8	8.8
Entrepreneurs with prior business experience(s) in the U.S. (N)	56	47	103
Sources of capital mobilization for prior businesses (%)			
Personal Savings	50.0	68.1	58.3
Social networks	8.9	12.8	10.7
Family networks	42.9	29.8	36.9
Bank loans	14.3	14.9	14.6
Money from Korea	21.4	12.8	17.5
RCA (Kye)	5.4	2.1	3.9
Little or no capital required	7.1	14.9	10.7

*Since interviewees had multiple sources of capital, the total percentage of
   capital sources for each groups is higher than 100%.

most owners used their personal savings. Therefore, the proportion of those who used personal savings as a capital source has been overestimated partially because some entrepreneurs start businesses with very low capital requirements or others with hardly any capital at all, and because they responded personal saving as a source of capital. In addition, some reported "owner financing" as personal savings, which also resulted in an overestimation of personal savings. An interviewee who established his business with his own capital said,

> I opened a business by using my own savings because the capital requirement was low for my first business. I started with a very small grocery and repeatedly sold and bought bigger ones. Also, one of reasons that I could start a business with little capital was through a

> system of "owner financing," which allowed me to down pay a small amount and have monthly payments until the rest was paid off. That is how I have reached the current size of business.

A doctor who opened a medical office with his own savings said,

> It requires little money to open a private medical office. Since I had worked as a resident and saved some of the earnings, I could manage to open an office using my own savings.

In addition, a large proportion of entrepreneurs use personal loans from friends, family, or relatives in addition to their own savings. A noticeable tendency is that for those who borrowed capital through personal loans, the amount of the loans to invest is higher than one's own savings, which creates circumstances that personal loans become a more important sources of business capital. The rate of entrepreneurs who started from borrowed money increases, especially when they started relatively larger businesses.

Unlike information mobilization for which social networks are a fundamental resource, an apparent tendency is that capital is mobilized through family networks far more frequently than social networks. That is, family networks become more pivotal for capital mobilization than social networks. In contrast to the argument of Goldberg (1985) that "capital circuits" are closely connected to the "information conduits," capital and information are generated from two completely different sources: family networks for capital and social networks for business information.

In addition, although numerous researchers for immigrant entrepreneurship (Aldrich and Zimmer, 1986; Light, 1972; Min, 1987; Waldinger, 1989; Wilson and Martin, 1982) have discovered the importance in the utilization of networks for resources, they did not separate family and social networks, nor did they investigate systemically which networks are useful to generate which resources. In other words, although previous studies acknowledge that networks are important and at times distinguish family networks and social networks, they neglect to investigate the details of these networks but conclude with a general perception that networks are decisive resources for immigrant entrepreneurship. As a result, the contemplation of networks tends to have resulted in incomplete conclusions for networks.

However, as tables 6-5 and 6-6 show, there is a definitive tendency regarding networks utilized for resource mobilization: family networks are more often used for capital mobilization; and social networks are more often used for information mobilization. The tendency is consistent regardless it is prior businesses or the current businesses. Although Werbner (1984) argues that an established trust in the community provides "sponsorship, patronage, credit, or advice" through social connections, Korean entrepreneurs do not seem to utilize social networks for capital provision as much as expected, even after living for a while in the community and establishing trust in the community.

On the other hand, non-college graduates tend to utilize social networks for capital provision more often than the counterparts. We can speculate from the tendency that the family of non-college graduates might be less successful economically and might not have enough capital to help the family start businesses. However, college graduates might have family members who are better off economically and able to help them with capital. Therefore, the important indication is that college graduates not only have social networks that furnish them with prompt trust in the community and information, but also family networks that help them with capital for business establishment. The superior sources of resource mobilization for the college graduates capacitate them to enter entrepreneurship easier and sooner than the non-college graduates, as shown in Chapter V.

College graduates have an intensive utilization of family networks for capital of prior businesses. Chain migrants with a college educational background utilized family networks pervasively for capital provision of the prior businesses. On the other hand, non-college graduates tend to utilize social networks for capital mobilization more frequently than college graduates for both the prior and current businesses. In addition, for both college graduates and non-college graduates, there is a general increase in the utilization of social networks for capital of the current businesses, which indicates that entrepreneurs establish social networks as they live longer in the community, and utilize the social networks for capital to establish the current businesses. Nonetheless, social networks remain a relatively insignificant source for capital mobilization.

In fact, a moderate level of social network utilization for capital mobilization is induced by the teenage migrants. Only teenage migrants are more prone to utilize social networks for capital provision since they have lived their adult life in the United States. That is, their lengthy residence in the United States allows them to have well established social networks to borrow capital for business establishments. In addition, despite the general lower utilization of social networks for capital provision, an increased rate of usage of social networks is higher among non-chain migrants, indicating that those without family or relatives to borrow money from tend to use social networks more actively for resource mobilization. Furthermore, considering that higher proportion of college graduates are non-chain migrants, college educational background seem to help them gaining business capital as well as information.

Money brought from Korea, on the other hand, was found to be important for business establishment (Min, 1996). The proportion of those who brought money from Korea at the time of immigration does not vary much on the basis of educational background: 34.5% of college graduates; 38.9% of non-college graduates. However, despite the significantly high proportion of those who brought money, the way in which they optimize the value of the money brought from Korea is largely dependent on educational background. As Table 6-6 indicates college graduates utilize money brought from Korea more contributory than non-college graduates for capital to start businesses. In addition, the responses are polarized between two extremes: "very useful" and "not useful at all." Among the interviewees who brought money from Korea at the time of immigration, 76.7% of college graduates responded that the money was "very useful" for start-up capital while 53.6% of the non-college graduates responded that the money was "very useful." Otherwise, the rest responded "not useful at all." In other words, college graduates maximize the usage of the money brought from Korea, whereas non-college graduates tend not to be capable of capitalizing the important assets.

The tendency that non-college graduates cannot as effectively optimize the usage of money brought from Korea was explained by an interviewee as follows:

> I brought money from Korea. But I could not find a suitable business to operate immediately. While I was looking for a chance to run a business, I needed money to make a living with my family. So, I spent most of the money I brought from Korea. I started a business bare handed.

As this interview reveals, networks established before or after immigration play a significant role, enabling newcomers to make use of their resources without wasting them. The utilization of money brought from Korea is the lowest among immigrants without a college education or family networks, which suggests that it is more difficult to make use of resources effectively to establish a business without the aid of either family networks or social networks. That is, without family networks or social networks, they are in an unfavorable situation not only for business establishment, but also in for utilization of assets.

Although the proportion of those who brought money from Korea is significant, the time of immigration is a indication of whether they brought enough capital to utilize for business establishment. The amount of money brought by the earlier immigrants is very small, hardly enough for a business establishment. The Korean immigrants who brought relatively large amounts of money to open businesses are only those who immigrated after the 1980s. That is, contrary to the general conception that Korean immigrants tend to bring money from Korea and establish businesses successfully with that money, the proportion of those who brought a large enough amount of money to open a business is smaller than expected. In addition, only those who immigrated after the 1980s brought a sufficient amount to invest in business establishment. The tendencies are illustrated by the following comment by an interviewee:

> In the 1960s and 1970s, immigrants were prohibited by the Korean government to take more than $5,000 per adult. So, the money that I brought from Korea was too little to invest for a business and was used up for making a living at the beginning. I could start a business only after working for a while and getting to know the Korean community and their business operations.

It also seems that personal borrowing is a more preferred method than institutionalized sources such as banks. However, the tendency can be understood by apprehending restricted situations that the entrepreneurs encounter. Korean immigrants are reluctant to get bank loans due to the lack of credit history, enormous amount of paper work, insufficient language skills, and unfamiliar loan systems. As a result, the entrepreneurs who utilize bank loans more frequently are those who have a higher educational background, who are chain-migrants with a family member to help them with paper work, or who have prior experiences in operating businesses utilizing bank loans. Therefore, the institutionalized loan system is more frequently used by those who have an access to gaining information on banks loans through family networks. In addition, the fact that Korean entrepreneurs utilize bank loans more often for their current businesses than for their prior businesses, suggests that the more familiar they get with the system as result of a longer term residence in the U.S., the more often they utilize the institutionalized system. Also, Korean entrepreneurs with prior experiences of business operation might have better chances of getting loans from banks due to accumulated credit histories.

Furthermore, researchers (Light, 1972; Light and Bonacich, 1988; Kim and Hurh, 1985; Portes and Manning, 1986; Light et al., 1990) consider that the rotating credit association (RCA: Kye) is a decisive resource of capital for Asian immigrants' business establishment and that it allows Asian immigrants to be competitive in entrepreneurship. Therefore, the RCA is recognized as a factor influencing social mobility for some Asian immigrants (Light et al., 1990). However, as Table 6-6 shows, the RCA is rarely used for capital provision either for the prior or the current businesses. As an interviewee who was involved in a RCA explains, the role of RCA for capital provision to establish businesses is not extensive, contrary to what has been argued. The interviewee says,

> I am involved in a Kye. But the money generated from the Kye is too small to be used for business establishment. The main purpose of being involved in a Kye association is to meet people, because we have a regular meeting once a month. At the meeting, I make friends as well as gain business information. Although money collected at the Kye is sometimes used for buying stocks for the business, it is mostly used for family affairs.

Counter to the belief that RCA contributes immensely to Korean entrepreneurs' business capital, among Korean immigrant entrepreneurs in Atlanta, RCA constitutes a rather minor portion of the sources of capital mobilization for business establishment. Then, are the findings of previous studies misleading? As Table 6-7 shows, RCA is a useful capital resource for further investment after businesses are established and a large proportion of Korean entrepreneurs rely on it.

Table 6-7: Utilization of Credit Rotating Associations for Korean Entrepreneurship (%)

	College graduates	Non-college graduates	Total
Total number of interviewees (N)	87	72	159
Entrepreneurs involved in RCA	43.7	65.3	53.5
Purposes of involving in RCA			
Friendship	37.8	27.7	32.1
Financing the current businesses	43.2	48.9	46.4
Importance of RCA for the current business operation			
Very important	34.2	40.4	37.6
Somewhat important	34.2	27.7	30.6
Not very important	0.0	8.5	4.7
Not import at all	31.6	23.4	27.1
Important in economic aspect	71.1	72.3	71.8
Important in social aspect	54.1	50.0	51.8

Although RCA is not utilized for start-up capital, RCA seems to be rather important for further investments after businesses are established. A large proportion of the interviewees are currently involved in a RCA with a much higher proportion of non-college graduate involvement. A large proportion of the entrepreneurs are involved in RCA for financing the current businesses, and a slightly lower proportion of them are involved for friendship. In addition, a very large proportion of the entrepreneurs consider RCA as a very important capital source for the current business operation and otherwise others do not utilize RCA for business capital at all. A very large proportion of the entrepreneurs consider it to be an important economic aspect, while a lower but still considerably large proportion of them consider it to be an important social aspect.

That is, although RCA is rarely used to start a business, capital accumulated through RCA is utilized for businesses in one way or another after the businesses are established, and regular RCA meetings are utilized for social network establishment. As a result, RCA is utilized more often and importantly for further investment in the current businesses, rather than for business establishments. Considering that entrepreneurs consistently need more capital during business operation, the fact that Korean entrepreneurs have a capital resource for further investment without going through immense paper work for bank loans, provides a competitive advantage to operate businesses over other ethnic or minority groups in the United States.

SUMMARY

Although previous studies found that class resources reflected by higher educational level constitute a valuable resource for immigrants to establish entrepreneurship (Bates, 1994a, 1997; Sanders and Nee, 1996; Yoon, 1991c), they do not discuss in detail how class resources convert into the resources necessary to help establish businesses. However, the analysis in this chapter shows that the class resources based on educational background play a decisive role in the establishment of social networks, which provide valuable resources for business establishment. Therefore, high educational background converts into resources for business establishment through social networks. Furthermore, Yoon (1991c) discovered in Chicago that educational level is decisive in the later stage of business development as the size of the business is larger. However, as the analysis in this chapter demonstrates, educational background is crucial from the starting point of business establishment through social networks, which facilitate the acquisition of valuable business information and connections in the community.

Moreover, considering that those with higher educational backgrounds have more dedicated and stronger social networks and most business information is acquired through social networks, those with higher educational backgrounds enter a better condition in which to start businesses and efficiently utilize resources such as money from Korea. Therefore, the fact that Korean immigrants with higher educational backgrounds start businesses sooner, often immediately after immigration appears to have been influenced by the social networks based on class resources. Therefore, class resources are indispensable for social network establishment and the social networks in the community profoundly help Korean immigrants in their pursuit of entrepreneurship. The social networks in the community enhance individual capacities to establish entrepreneurship because they are crucial for generating resources for business establishment.

In addition, this analysis shows an explicit difference in the utilization of social and family networks, in that Korean entrepreneurs rely on family networks more for monetary resources and social networks for business information. This separate contemplation of social and family networks shows how the different characteristics of these networks operate differently to generate different resources. In general, a separate examination of networks helps us to better understand how they are utilized.

Traditional beliefs have been that ethnic resources allow Asian immigrants to become more successful and more prone to be entrepreneurs (Kim and Hurh, 1985). Often times, the ethnic resources include unpaid family labor, frugal attitudes, hard work, or RCA. However, these ethnic resources are not so crucial for business establishment as they are for business operation, which will be further discussed in Chapter VII. Among ethnic resources, this analysis clearly shows that RCA is much more important for business operation rather than business establishment. Therefore, the ethnic resources are important by giving a competitive advantage over other ethnic or minority groups who do not utilize them. In addition, ethnic resources should be contemplated separately from social networks and family networks instead of being lumped into one concept, since these resources operate distinctively according to their individual characteristics.

As the importance of the utilization of social networks and family networks for business establishments are examined, the utilization of ethnic resources will be examined in next chapter to uncover how ethnic resources provide advantages for Korean business operations. In addition, the next chapter will examine how mobilized resources through family networks and social networks lead Korean entrepreneurs into different economic niches: the enclave and non-enclave economies.

CHAPTER VII

Networks and Ethnic Resources

Korean immigrant entrepreneurs tend to enter into two economic niches: the enclave economy catering to Korean customers; and the non-enclave economy catering mainly to inner city African-American customers and some middle class white customers. Therefore, a variety of resources that immigrant entrepreneurs utilize and factors that immigrants encounter in the host society are examined simultaneously to comprehend differing paths of ethnic entrepreneurship and how entrepreneurs choose which economic niches in the ethnic economy to enter.

In general, however, previous researches of immigrant entrepreneurship have tended to examine such factors as social networks, ethnic resources, and economic structures separately and, as a result, overlook the dynamics of immigrant entrepreneurship. Structural influences on immigrant entrepreneurship cannot be examined without connections to entrepreneurs' individual resources, just as entrepreneurs' personal advantages cannot be examined without considering the position of immigrant entrepreneurship in the larger economic structure.

Therefore, this chapter first examines how individual resources and economic structures interact to help Korean immigrant entrepreneurs develop along different paths into enclave and non-enclave businesses. Second, it examines how significant role ethnic resources plays in each of the economic niches and how ethnic resources are utilized by Korean immigrant entrepreneurs to stay competitive in entrepreneurship. These questions will be examined together by comprehending the interaction between structural resources and individual resources.

ADVANTAGES IN THE ECONOMIC STRUCTURE

Previous investigations have shown that there are advantageous economic factors which can create an environment that helps ethnic entrepreneurship emerge. Bonacich (1973) and Waldinger and Aldrich (1990) argue that the larger economic structure has a gap that there is a market which is left un- or under-served by the mainstream economy due partially to high crime rates and low profit margin. In addition, since the size of the industry within this gap is small, its market performance fluctuates more than does the general economy. When market performance fluctuates due to unstable demand, and when an industry does not generate a large profit due to its small size, large corporations are not attracted to the economy, leaving opportunities for those with smaller amounts of capital. Therefore, this structural gap becomes a structural advantage that immigrants can fit into as a "middleman minority" and enables immigrant entrepreneurship to emerge (Morokvasic et al., 1990; Bonacich, 1973). These industries provide an opportunity for immigrants who lack capital and information, and who are willing to endure a harsh working environment. Since this market is a vacuum area that is seldom served by larger firms, potential entrepreneurs such as immigrants who lack resources take advantage of the low competition from larger firms and make use of the opportunities.

Another market available is the enclave economy in which immigrants are concentrated (Portes and Manning, 1986). This market is available only for the ethnic entrepreneurs who offer unique cultural products to a concentrated ethnic population. In the enclave economy, there are reciprocal and paternalistic relationships between immigrant entrepreneurs and coethnic workers: immigrant entrepreneurs provide job opportunities to coethnic workers; and workers provide a cheap source of labor (Wilson and Portes, 1980; Portes and Manning, 1986). In this economic relationship, workers learn and develop skills for the purpose operating businesses of their own in the future. Further, since the enclave economy is unique in terms of the products and services it caters, it is insulated from other ethnic members or from the mainstream society, which gives competitive advantages to both coethnic entrepreneurs and workers. Therefore, Light and his colleagues (Light et al., 1993; Light and Karageorgis, 1994; Light et al., 1994) define both industries in the enclave economy and outside it operated by immigrants as the "ethnic economy."

Despite that the structures are presumably available for all ethnic groups, only certain immigrant groups are likely to establish small businesses and move up in the socio-economic hierarchy (Hoffman and Marger, 1991). Given these economic structures, whether or not an immigrant group develops an entrepreneurial capability is largely dependent on how immigrants capitalize the economic structure in combination with personal resources. That is, assuming that the structural advantages are available for all immigrant groups, a varying capacity to transform structural advantages into resources as well as to generate personal resources that can be utilized in individual economic pursuits would cause a difference in the rate of participation in entrepreneurship among different ethnic groups.

Considering that Korean immigrants have one of the highest proportions of self-employed entrepreneurs (Bonacich and Jung, 1982; Light and Bonacich, 1988; Portes and manning, 1986; Waldinger and Aldrich, 1990), and that, as was examined in the earlier chapters, Korean entrepreneurs utilize class resources and social and/or family networks to establish businesses, the existing economic structure can be advantageous only for those ethnic groups who are capable to generate or possess personal resources such as networks and ethnic resources. The economic structure of Atlanta is the same as it is in other cities where Korean immigrants are concentrated: namely, the enclave economy that caters to Korean customers; and the non-enclave economy that caters to the majority of customers in inner city neighborhoods, as well as a small proportion that caters to residents of middle class neighborhoods. In pursuit of entrepreneurship, the first decision for Korean immigrants to make is between types of businesses, whether they should cater to Korean customers or to non-Korean customers. As a result, Korean entrepreneurs pursue different paths of entrepreneurship either in the enclave or non-enclave on the basis of the resources that they can possess or generate. These resources will be examined in detail in the next section.

Among the Korean immigrant entrepreneurs interviewed in Atlanta, 76.1% have experienced living in other cities in the U.S. after immigration. The motivations of those who moved to Atlanta from other cities are mainly related to expectations of better economic opportunities in businesses or jobs. The presence of family members or friends in Atlanta also encouraged many to move to Atlanta, because their family members or friends provided information regarding opportunities in businesses and jobs. However, the information, such as crime rates, may have been partially misleading due to their unfamiliarity of the society. For instance, one interviewee said,

> I have a sister in Atlanta. She told me that opportunities in businesses for black customers are better in Atlanta, because of lower crime rates. Businesses for black customers have been in a downfall for a long time since the 1980s when the government cut welfare. Since Atlanta is going to host the Olympics, I expected economic performance might be better than in other cities.

On the other hand, the enclave businesses seem to have emerged in Atlanta due to a drastic increase in the Korean population in Atlanta. Although the residential areas of Korean immigrants are scattered around the Atlanta area, the enclave economy catering to the Korean population is established in a north-eastern part of Atlanta. A long-time resident in Atlanta said,

> We first started businesses on Buford Highway because the rent was cheap, due to the area's remoteness from downtown. The current Korea Town originally was a residential area for blacks with a few Chinese residents. Once Korean businesses moved into the area, the Korean population outnumbered all populations around this area and developed a Korean economic niche. As Korea Town became vivid in the area, more Korean immigrants were attracted here, which increased the size of Korea Town. I think it is good to have a Korea Town for entrepreneurs like me. Since most Korean products and services are concentrated in this area, it becomes a center for Korean activity and draws more people to the area to meet others, to buy Korean products, or to get services like restaurants, doctors, and accountants in the Korean way.

In addition, those with employment experience in the enclave economy in other cities naturally look for business opportunities in the enclave economy in Atlanta. As a restaurant owner said,

> I worked as a cook at a Korean-Japanese restaurant in New York for about 10 years. After I had saved a good sum of money, I began to look for a business to operate myself. However, the rent for a restaurant was extremely high in New York so I could not afford it. In the mean time, I heard that the Korean community in Atlanta was

growing and that business opportunities in Atlanta were good. So, I moved to Atlanta where it is cheaper to open a business. However, even in Atlanta, my savings were not enough to open a well-founded restaurant. So, I met people who were in a similar situation. We collected money and invested in the Korean restaurant that we have now. We have the best business in Korea Town.

Therefore, considering that Korean entrepreneurs find business opportunities in two economic niches in the enclave for Korean customers or the non-enclave for African-American customers, the existence of the two economic niches evidently provides business opportunities for Korean entrepreneurs. However, the structural advantage is only available when they have sources for business information.

However, as far as the structural factors are considered, structural advantages ought to be considered along with structural disadvantages. The consideration of structural disadvantages helps to explain the reason why Korean immigrants look for business or job opportunities in the enclave or non-enclave in the inner city neighborhood economies rather than in the mainstream economy. Immigrants are essentially excluded from the mainstream for both job and entrepreneurial opportunities, because the capital requirement for business establishment is far too high in the mainstream economy, because discrimination plays a role in the labor market, and because English skills are limited.

Most entrepreneurs seem to have experienced limited opportunities for business operation. That is, the majority of interviewees indicated that they found limited opportunities for operating businesses in the mainstream economy for catering to white middle class customers and for getting jobs or promotional chances in the mainstream labor market. They are unable to get into the mainstream economy due to a lack of resources such as information and capital. Their limited opportunities for getting into the mainstream economy, therefore, encouraged them to get into un- or under-severed markets, which primarily exist in the Korean community and in the inner city minority neighborhoods. The majority of interviewees in the non-enclave economy made observations similar to the following:

Where else could I open a business? If I open a business in the white neighborhood, they would not come into the store because it is owned by some foreigner, an immigrant. Most of all, I do not have enough money to open a business in a middle class neighborhood with mostly white customers, because the businesses in those neighborhoods require far more capital than one would need to open one in an inner city neighborhood. Moreover, small shops cannot compete with the large franchise stores. The reason why we can survive here is because most black residents do not have cars and need to buy groceries nearby. Also, black customers do not mind about the race of shop owners, unlike white customers. I want to change my business to cater to middle class customers and I don't want to serve low class customers any more, because it is just too tough to deal with customers here. I do not care about the race of customers as long as they are middle class, then customers would not be as tough as they are here. It is also very dangerous to run businesses in these neighborhoods because often there are violent crimes and shop owners get shot to death.

Another interviewee says the following:

It is easier to start a business for black customers than for white customers because of a lower requirement in capital. I would not be able to start a business in a shopping mall where whites are the majority of customers, because rent is very expensive there. On the contrary, it is possible for me to open a business in a black area because the rent is cheap. In addition, white customers might care about the race of the shop owner and be picky, whereas it is easy to serve black customers because they are not picky. With a limited amount of capital, the only businesses available are those in the black neighborhoods. If I change my business, I would like to change it to serve the middle class customers because of the safety reason. If I serve middle class customers, it would not only be easier to deal with customers, but I would also make more money in richer neighborhoods than in the poor neighborhoods here.

Therefore, an interaction among three factors (i.e., available structural opportunities in the minority neighborhood, limited opportunities in the general market, and limited capital) encourages Korean immigrants to pursue entrepreneurship in inner city neighborhoods. In other words, in the situation in which business opportunities for the general market and capital are limited, Korean immigrants tend to pursue entrepreneurship in the black neighborhoods where market opportunities are available and the capital requirements are lower.

On the other hand, although entrepreneurs in the enclave economy seem to experience the same difficulty as those in the non-enclave economy with entering the mainstream economy, they seem to have even lower capital than those in the non-enclave economy, in general. That is, between the two available markets that Korean entrepreneurs can occupy, those with less capital tend to pursue businesses in the enclave economy, which will be shown in the next section.

Therefore, an interaction between two economic structures, a structure with a limitation and a structure with an opportunity, allow Korean immigrants to get into entrepreneurship. In other words, the limited opportunities in the mainstream economy compel Korean immigrants to search for available opportunities, which are located in the enclave and non-enclave in the inner city neighborhoods, with a few in the middle-class neighborhoods. Furthermore, their individual capacities to mobilize resources divides Korean immigrants into two economic niches, the enclave and non-enclave. The sources of resource mobilization will be examined in the next section of this chapter.

BUSINESSES IN THE ETHNIC ECONOMY

Table 7-1 shows general traits of Korean businesses in Atlanta. The ethnic economy is divided into two economic niches, enclave and non-enclave, in which most Korean entrepreneurs operate their businesses. The length of time running the current businesses indicates stability of businesses. As Aldrich and Auster (1986) found, non-enclave businesses tend to be owned by one owner for a longer period than do the enclave businesses. Considering that the length of time running the current businesses is significantly longer among the non-enclave businesses, non-enclave businesses are more stable than are enclave businesses and the failure rate in the non-enclave economy is lower.

In addition, the length of time running the current businesses has another implication that Korean entrepreneurs often sell their current businesses and move on to bigger businesses after they accumulate more capital and experience in the business. Therefore, until they reach the point where business is substantially large and stable, Korean entrepreneurs keep selling small business and buying bigger business.

Table 7-1: General Traits of the Current Businesses in the Korean Ethnic Economy

	Enclave businesses	Non-enclave businesses	Total
Total number of interviewees (N)	70	89	159
Length of time running the current businesses (yrs.)	2.82 (2.08)*	5.03 (3.83)*	
Amount invested ($)	35,000 *	$90,000 *	
Own multiple businesses (%)	17.1	30.3	24.5
Annual gross sales (%)			
Under $30,000	4.3	3.4	3.8
$30,000-$49,999	17.1	4.5	10.1
$50,000-$99,999	27.1	7.9	16.4
$100,000-$299,999	24.3	29.2	27.0
$300,000-$499,999	10.0	25.8	18.9
$500,000-$999,999	2.9	11.2	7.5
$1,000,000 or more	10.0	14.6	12.6
Number of employees in the current business(es) (%)			
No employees	34.3	18.0	25.2
1 or 2 employees	37.1	32.6	34.6
3 to 5 employees	12.9	23.6	18.9
More than 6 employees	15.7	25.8	21.4
Intend to move economic niches (%)	46.3	59.5	53.6

*Median

Therefore, although often times a short length of time has an implication of failure, a shorter length should not be interpreted solely as failure.

As shown in Table 7-1, the amount invested in the current businesses shows that businesses in the non-enclave tend to require much higher capital than those in the enclave economy. However, the figure of the investment of starting the businesses is slightly overestimated because some included the amount of "owner's financing" in their total investment. Given the two economic niches available and the larger requirement of capital in the non-enclave economy, the capacity for business capital mobilization is one of the crucial factors that divides Korean entrepreneurs between the enclave and non-enclave.

Considering annual gross sales and the number of employees, there is a consistent indication that non-enclave businesses are more prosperous in size and economic performance. For instance, the non-enclave businesses tend to have a moderate sales volume: the majority of non-enclave businesses have over $100,000 of sales volume, whereas more than a half of enclave businesses have either middle range or lower sales volume. In addition, despite that a large proportion of Korean businesses have no or a couple of employees, businesses in the non-enclave economy tend to be larger in size in that a higher proportion of non-enclave businesses employ more than three employees.

It is a general perception of Korean immigrants that non-enclave businesses catering to other minorities are the only alternative opportunity open to them with relatively better economic returns than the businesses in the enclave economy. Based on the higher sales volume available to the businesses in the non-enclave economic niche, entrepreneurs consider the non-enclave businesses a better opportunity for Korean immigrants. Therefore, enclave businesses more often fit the typical image of mom-and-pop shops run by wives and husbands, perhaps employing only one or two workers. On the other hand, non-enclave businesses tend to be larger with more employees and more prosperous with a higher sales volume.

Given the economic niches in the enclave and non-enclave, a large proportion of Korean entrepreneurs, regardless of the economic niches, intend to move their businesses closer to the mainstream economy. For instance, inasmuch as a large proportion of non-enclave entrepreneurs in the inner city want to move their businesses into more prosperous neighborhoods, a large proportion of entrepreneurs in the enclave also want to move out or expand their market to the mainstream economy for better economic returns and opportunities. In addition, given that the businesses in the non-enclave are more prosperous than those in the enclave, a lot of entrepreneurs in the enclave also want to move into the non-enclave businesses in the inner city. Although the majority of Korean entrepreneurs occupy economic niches either in Korea Town or in the inner city neighborhoods, those opportunities are not abundant and are not satisfactory due to lack of long-term economic prospects and low margins. Moreover, although the businesses in the non-enclave are larger and more prosperous than those in the enclave economy, business owners in the non-enclave economic niches want to move to other economic niches due to low profit margins and high crime rates.

For example, entrepreneurs in the enclave economy tend to have a desire to move to the non-enclave economy where economic return is higher, whereas entrepreneurs in the non-enclave economy tend to desire to move to an economy that is safer than the inner city African-American neighborhoods. In addition, entrepreneurs in both economic niches desire to move into an economy that serves middle class customers since this economy is larger and more prosperous. As a result, a majority of entrepreneurs want to move their businesses away from their current situations or expand to the market of the general population. As one wholesaler said,

> Since my store is located in Korea Town, I used to have only Korean retailers as customers, who have businesses in downtown areas catering to black customers. However, I expanded to black and Asian Indian customers, who also have businesses in the same area. Problems for the businesses in Korea Town are that the market is too limited and that the businesses are too competitive among Korean business owners. The competition undermines the prices and induces a lower margin. In the future, I would like to change the type of the business and move the business itself to white neighborhoods, where the profit margin is higher. Right now, I do not have any specific plan about the type or location of a new business. I also know it will be very difficult for Koreans as immigrants to overcome the barrier of white markets. But once a business settles down, a business catering to white customers will have a better margin and I can expect a long term prospect.

As an alternative to the businesses in the enclave or in the inner city neighborhoods, dry cleaning stores, which are mostly located in middle class neighborhoods or offices, seem to be considered the only opportunity by which Korean immigrants can run businesses for white or middle class customers. As an owner of a dry cleaning store said,

> When I was looking for business sites, I did not care about the race of customers. I instead paid more attention to the income level of the neighborhoods. Although the dry cleaning business is labor intensive like other businesses, requiring an equal level of hard work, I preferred this type of business because of safety reasons. In the middle-class neighborhood, the customers are not as tough as the inner city customers and I do not need to deal with customers for

tedious matters. I want to change my business to something that requires less labor, because this kind of business is too labor intensive.

Given that non-enclave businesses catering to inner city customers tend to have higher economic returns and that opportunities for businesses in the mainstream economy are limed, Korean immigrants tend to pursue non-enclave businesses. However, Korean entrepreneurs are clearly divided into two economic niches based on the ethnicity of customers. The higher capital investments necessary for businesses in the non-enclave economy requires business owners in the non-enclave to generate more resources than those in the enclave. Considering that businesses owners desire to enter into the non-enclave economy that is more prosperous, raising capital seems to be crucial for occupancy of economic niches with better economic returns. Entrepreneurs in the enclave economy, therefore, seem to experience further constraints on business operation and opportunities due to a shortage of capital. The following sections will examine how the two economic structures coincide with individual capacities of resource generation to divide Korean entrepreneurs into two economic niches.

UTILIZATION OF NETWORKS IN THE ETHNIC ECONOMY

Table 7-2 shows sources of resource mobilization that Korean entrepreneurs used for entering economic niches either in the enclave or the non-enclave economy. The general perception is that capital is the most crucial resource for business establishment regardless whether they are disadvantaged as immigrants and women or privileged as the majority. According to interviewees, however, it seems that capital is not the only prominent requirement for business establishment, but business information is another crucial resource to start businesses in the economic niches with better return. The vast majority of entrepreneurs in the non-enclave economy collected their business information through social networks or employment experiences in the U.S., which is another form of social networks.

Therefore, social networks established in the community are critical for obtaining the valuable information that enables Korean entrepreneurs to get into the non-enclave economy where businesses are more stable and lucrative. An interviewee who received help from his friends in deciding what type of business to start said,

Table 7-2: Utilization of Networks for Korean Entrepreneurship (%)

	Enclave businesses	Non-enclave businesses	Total
Total number of interviewees (N)	70	89	159
Source of information			
Social networks	22.9	47.2	36.5
Family networks	10.0	13.5	11.9
Employment experiences in the U.S.	18.6	40.5	30.8
Skills from Korea	24.3	3.4	12.6
Prior business experiences	8.6	13.5	11.3
Professional background	12.9	4.5	8.2
Source of capital provision			
Personal Savings	57.1	83.1	71.7
Social networks	14.3	16.9	15.7
Family networks	28.6	31.5	30.2
Bank loans	17.1	29.2	23.9
Money from Korea	21.4	18.0	19.5
RCA (Kye)	5.7	10.1	8.2
Little capital required	14.3	4.5	8.8
Types of organization involved			
Korean churches	70.0	53.9	61.0
Alumni associations	17.1	15.7	16.4
Community associations	14.3	10.1	11.9
Business associations	12.9	27.0	20.8
Hobby clubs	8.6	5.6	6.9
None	12.9	19.1	16.4

> Although I wanted to start a grocery, I did not know about business operation nor management. So, I started a business as a partnership with my friend who has experience in the grocery business. While running the business, I learned to operate and maintain the grocery business. After learning from the partnership, I started my own business.

Another interviewee said,

> The priest of my church asked me to move to Atlanta because the environment for businesses and the living conditions are better in

Atlanta than those big cities due to the lower crime rate. When I moved to Atlanta, my priest recommended to run a convenience store. After I investigated those businesses, I found the businesses are unsatisfactory due to unstable economic returns. In the mean time, I had a friend who owned several beauty supply stores in the black neighborhoods. I helped my friend, so that I could learn the business. After a while, I bought two beauty supply stores myself in another black neighborhood. I prefer this type of business because it does not require extra long hours of work.

Therefore, considering that a large proportion of Korean entrepreneurs accumulate business skills with the help of friends, social networks through employment experience at Korean businesses is a decisive resource for Korean entrepreneurship. While employed, they not only learn skills to start the same type of businesses, but also establish social networks that eventually become a profound resource to establish their businesses. The established social networks during employment in Korean businesses enable them to accumulate trust, which later helps their business establishments.

Considering the importance of social networks for business establishment and for getting into an economic niche with better economic returns, the individual capacity for establishing social networks seems to determine whether Korean entrepreneurs go into the enclave or the non-enclave. Yoon (1991c) found educational background is crucial at a later stage when businesses reach a large size. However, social networks are decisive for entering businesses with higher economic returns and, as shown in Chapter VI, educational background was crucial for social network establishment. Thus, educational background in conjunction with social networks play a crucial role from the onset of Korean entrepreneurship and during every aspect of it.

In contrast to the non-enclave businesses, although social networks for businesses in the enclave are also an important source of information mobilization, skills from Korea are a rather crucial resource for entrepreneurs in the enclave economy to establish their businesses. Therefore, entrepreneurs who immigrated with technical skills have the advantage of being able to start businesses in the enclave, since these skills are suitable to cater to Korean customers as they did in Korea. As a result, unlike the non-enclave businesses, business information acquired from social networks becomes far less important for entrepreneurs who intend to start businesses in the enclave. Therefore, enclave businesses tend to be established based on demands in the community rather than by utilizing information generated from social networks. A large portion of interviewees in the enclave economy expressed views similar with the following:

> I opened a video shop because there were no such businesses in Atlanta at the time when I opened. It is only very recently that a lot of video rental shops have opened. Since Korean immigrants are still fond of Korean soap operas, comedies, and music shows, this kind of shop is in great demand.

Therefore, entrepreneurs in the enclave economy seem to have the advantage of familiarity with Korean cultural tastes and preferences.

Korean immigrants in Atlanta, especially those with the experience of living in other cities, know where the opportunities are for Korean entrepreneurship in the enclave and non-enclave economic niches. Moreover, 64.8% of interviewees became immigrants after the 1980s, when the Korean immigrant economy in the U.S. was well established in the form of businesses in the enclave in the Korean community and in the non-enclave in the inner city; and they also immigrated with the intention of operating businesses. This tendency increases the likelihood of Korean immigrants getting into businesses. In particular, those with knowledge of the business opportunities in the enclave or the non-enclave are likely to have pursued these opportunities on the basis of information they obtained. Therefore, considering that the Korean community in Atlanta become large and vitalized in the late 1980s, it is not a coincidence that the community members in Atlanta established the same economic structures that Koreans in other cities have established.

Chapter VI shows that entrepreneurs' personal savings and family networks (i.e., loans from family or relatives) are the leading sources of capital provision, regardless of economic niches. Personal savings are a more significant source of business capital for the non-enclave businesses, which indicates that entrepreneurs need to have their own capital at a certain level to start non-enclave businesses. The tendency is because the higher requirement of capital for the non-enclave businesses create circumstances such that only those who are already rich could start businesses in that economic niche. Again, Table 7-2 shows that it is evident that family networks are an important source for capital mobilization, in that a large proportion of Korean entrepreneurs regardless of economic niches borrowed money from their family or relatives.

However, since the non-enclave businesses require higher capital than the enclave businesses, a high proportion of entrepreneurs in the non-enclave economy utilizes institutionalized loans (i.e., banks) more often than the enclave businesses do. That is, since they can generate only a limited amount capital from family or friends, those who operate larger businesses tend to utilize bank loans as a source of capital. Therefore, those who have prior business experiences have a better chance to start a business in the non-enclave economy due partially to their accumulated business experience, and partially to the accumulated credit history which provides them an access to a large sum of capital through bank loans.

Money brought from Korea seems to be slightly more important for the enclave businesses than the non-enclave. The tendency might be due to the lower requirement of capital in the enclave economy, since in most cases the amount of capital brought from Korea is not sufficient enough to start a business that requires high capital. In addition, countering the general expectations, RCA (Kye) is not such a crucial source of capital for a business establishment in Atlanta, regardless of economic niches. Further, service businesses in the enclave such as real estate, insurance, or institutions for art or language lessons hardly need any capital to start compared with retail businesses, the low capital requirement is another important reason why immigrants start businesses in the enclave.

With regard to involvement in organizations, church seems to be particularly important for the entrepreneurs in the enclave, in that an overwhelmingly high proportion of entrepreneurs in the enclave economy are involved in churches in the Korean community. As shown in Chapter VI, churches are places where entrepreneurs meet people who eventually become customers. Therefore, churches seem to attract the entrepreneurs in the enclave economy more often than those in the non-enclave economy. On the other hand, a large proportion of entrepreneurs in the non-enclave are also involved in churches that generate business resources such as information. An interviewee noted as a reflection of this tendency,

> I do not go to a Korean church. Instead, I go to an American church because I see Korean immigrants' secular interests related to

businesses. They seem to come to church to run businesses there. I
want to be religious in church, rather than become a business person.

This tendency has become common knowledge in the community.
Although I cannot enumerate precisely, during the interviews quite a
large proportion of Koreans mentioned that they started going to church
after immigration, because they can make friends there, because they
can collect resources for further economic pursuits, and because they
can expand the number of customers. Business associations are more
popular for the entrepreneurs in the non-enclave economy, since most
business associations are relevant to the types of businesses catering to
non-Korean customers such as grocery stores, liquor stores, and dry
cleaning/coin laundry stores. Contrary to the non-enclave, businesses in
the enclave economy do not form business associations. The reason for
the tendency, that the non-enclave business entrepreneurs form
associations, may be that associations represent the interests of the
members in the larger society (e.g., security of their businesses in the
inner city neighborhoods).

Therefore, information collected through social networks is crucial
for entering businesses with higher economic returns, whereas capital
borrowed from family networks are crucial for businesses in both
economies. Moreover, the non-enclave businesses which require high
start-up capital tend to utilize institutional loan system from banks.

Once a business is established, entrepreneurs need resources to stay
competitive with other businesses. Under the circumstances, ethnic
resources play a significant role that helps Korean entrepreneurs
maintain and manage their businesses more competitively. These ethnic
resources will be examined in the following section.

UTILIZATION OF ETHNIC RESOURCES

Immigrants tend to come to a new society with ethnic traits such as a
frugal attitude, unpaid family labor, and ethnic solidarity as well as
class resources such as capital. These traits are considered to become
important resources for becoming competitive in business operations
(Light, 1984, 1985; Waldinger, 1979; Werbner, 1984). However,
although researchers agree that ethnic resources are important factors
for immigrants to be successful in businesses, they tend to generalize

that ethnic resources are useful in all stages of business. Therefore, ethnic resources will be discussed to find out how they are important once a business is established to stay competitive rather than to establish businesses.

Table 7-3 reveals that elements of ethnic resources such as frugal and hard working attitude, utilization of family networks, and the structural advantage in the ethnic economy. As Table 7-3 indicates, store hours and percentages of stores open on Saturdays and Sunday do not vary much between businesses in the enclave and non-enclave, because Korean entrepreneurs, in general, work extremely long hours regardless of economic niches and stay open even on weekends. To stay competitive, especially in the non-enclave economy, entrepreneurs said that they could not afford to close on weekends in order not to lose regular customers, since there are many more stores in the neighborhood. However, there is a large variation among the enclave businesses, in that professionals, travel or insurances agencies, and institutions for various lessons open relatively shorter hours, whereas most retail businesses and restaurants stay open excessively long hours. On the other hand, most of the non-enclave businesses stay open very long hours without having weekends off.

In addition, a large portion of Korean immigrant entrepreneurs work even after the store is closed. As the "Owners who work after hours" indicates, the entrepreneurs utilize the time after closing for organizing their stores and shelving stocks. As a result, considering the store hours and over work hours, a large proportion of the entrepreneurs work over 70 to 80 hours per week, which is much longer than ordinary office works in the United States. The excessively long working hours indicate that Korean immigrant entrepreneurs try to compensate their disadvantages through frugal altitudes and hard work.

A large portion of Korean businesses are small without any employees, and they tend to rely heavily on unpaid family labor. As a result, family labor has been considered an asset that provides competitive advantages (Bonacich et al., 1980; Kim and Hurh, 1985; Waldinger, 1989). Even in businesses with employees, family labor plays a significant role for the management and maintenance of businesses. Unpaid family labor is utilized more often among entrepreneurs in the non-enclave economy than those in the enclave. In addition, family labor in non-enclave business is considered more

Table 7-3: Utilization of Ethnic Resources

	Enclave businesses	Non-enclave businesses	Total
Total number of interviewees (N)	70	89	159
Average hours of stores opened (hrs./wk.)	60.0	66.1	
	58.2*	65.0*	
Saturdays open (%)	67.1	83.1	76.1
Sundays open (%)	37.1	32.6	34.6
Owners who work after hours (%)	64.3	31.5	45.9
Average hours of over work (hrs./wk.)	12.8	10.3	
	10.0*	10.0*	
Family labor utilized (%)	54.3	69.7	62.9
Hours of family labor (hrs./wk.)	40.4	43.8	
	40.0*	40.0*	
Importance of family labor (%)	65.8	79.0	74.0
Family members who work as unpaid labor (%)			
Spouse	84.2	80.6	82.0
Children	31.6	29.0	30.0
Parents	5.3	9.7	8.0
Siblings	5.3	8.1	7.0
Relatives	5.3	1.6	3.0
Bought an established businesses (%)	22.9	62.9	45.3
Bought from Korean prior owners (%)	56.3	64.3	62.5
Rotating Credit Associations (RCA: Kye) (%)			
Those Involved in RCA	50.0	56.2	53.5
Involved for an economic reason	80.0	66.0	71.8
Involved for a social reason	51.4	52.1	51.8
Finance the current business(es)	52.9	42.0	46.4

*Median

important than those in the enclave. The tendency is because service businesses in the enclave economy such as lawyers, accountants, travel agents, or insurance agents utilize family labor far less than other businesses.

However, when the unpaid family labor is used, regardless of economic niches family members also tend to work long hours on the top of the long hours that entrepreneurs work. On the other hand, although hours of family labor are almost the same regardless of economic niche, entrepreneurs in the non-enclave economy tend to cite the importance of family labor more frequently than those in the enclave. That is, family labor plays a more important role for the businesses in the non-enclave economy than those in the enclave economy.

The most commonly used family labor force is the spouses of entrepreneurs. The involvement of spouses in businesses seems to be indispensable, especially for the businesses in the non-enclave economy where the operating hours of most businesses are very long. As an interviewee in the non-enclave economy said,

> I cannot run this grocery without my wife. She is the only person whom I can rely on, whether or not I am present at this grocery. When I go out for buying merchandise, I need a very reliable person who can manage employees and deal with money. My wife takes all those responsibilities. She also works from open to close with me. I cannot expect any employee to work with me from open to close. So, we have a division of labor in that I deal with things outside of the business such as buying merchandise, and my wife deals with everything inside of the business such as cash registering, bookkeeping, and management of employees.

In addition, a female interviewee in the non-enclave economy who runs a clothing store said,

> My husband contributes a lot to this store, although he does not operate the store himself. He always goes out to buy stocks, while I operate the store. In this way, I do not need to go out and deal with American wholesalers with my limited English skills. My husband is an American, whom I met in Korea.

It seems, however, that although all spouses who work are considered "very important," those whose businesses are larger and settled in management tend to work shorter hours than those whose businesses are small in size.

Previous studies have found that although the patterns are different from city to city, "ecological succession" in the ethnic economy is an advantageous resource for immigrant entrepreneurship. The most commonly cited "ecological succession" is in Chicago, which occurred as the residential population changed from white to black after the massive in-migration of the black population into the Chicago area. A result was the abandonment of business sites and the turnover of businesses from white to black or Puerto Ricans in the early part of the century (Aldrich, 1975; Aldrich and Reiss, Jr., 1975), as well as to some Koreans during the civil rights era (Yoon, 1991b). Timely in-migration into the area secured opportunities for opening businesses in Chicago. In addition, it is argued that a vertical integration between Korean wholesaler and retailers is advantageous for Korean businesses, in that Korean wholesalers provide advantageous prices and information to the Korean retailers, whereas the retailers become a steady supply of customers for the Korean wholesalers (Yoon, 1991b).

Another form of ecological succession observed in Los Angeles is that Korean enterprises are exclusively sold to other Korean entrepreneurs (Light and Bonacich, 1988: Ch. 9). Over 80% of the Korean liquor stores in Los Angeles are sold to other Korean immigrants. In this way, entrepreneurs starting businesses for the first time take advantage of an established business site. In addition, vertical integration between Korean retailers and Korean wholesalers has been observed as a favorable factor for Korean entrepreneurship in inner city neighborhoods (Kim and Hurh, 1985; Yoon, 1991b).

However, the advantage of ecological succession is not a strong factor for entrepreneurship in Atlanta, as shown in the category "Bought an established businessses" in Table 7-3. The structural advantages above—timely in-migration, the selling of businesses to other Koreans, and vertical integration—are irrelevant to Korean entrepreneurship in Atlanta because: (1) the Atlanta Korean community has expanded to its current size fairly recently, since the end of the 1980s and, as a result, there was no timely in-migration like that which occurred in Chicago; (2) although some interviewees bought established businesses and some even bought them from Koreans, ecological succession is not nearly as significant as in Los Angeles, where the history of Korean immigration is long and the Korean community has been established for decades; and (3) vertical integration is only applicable for such businesses as wig, clothing, or shoe stores, and is not applicable to the major types of business in Atlanta such as grocery, liquor, and dry cleaning stores, because they do not have such advantages as vertical integration between Korean retailers and American wholesalers. In addition, businesses in the enclave economy rarely have such advantages because a large portion of businesses is in the service sector, such as restaurants, travel, insurance, and real estate agencies, and law and accounting firms.

However, although the evidence for ecological succession of businesses in Atlanta is rather weak, businesses in the non-enclave economy display more business succession by coethnic members than those in the enclave. Although a high proportion of entrepreneurs bought businesses from other Koreans, ecological succession among coethnic business members is only a recent trend in Atlanta. Most of the ecological succession occurred within the past several years. Although the effects of ecological succession are relatively minor compared to other cities, an importance of the ecological succession of businesses is social networks that are more pervasive in the non-enclave economy.

The ecological succession is further evidence for social networks. As Table 7-3 shows, although ecological succession of Korean entrepreneurs in Atlanta is not as significant a feature as in other cities, it occurs in relation to social networks. That is, entrepreneurs who bought businesses from Korean prior owners tend to have purchased the businesses through an introduction by other Korean business owners or by recommendation of their friends. However, social networks based on ecological succession are far less important for businesses in the enclave economy. Since the history of the Korean community in Atlanta is short, most enclave businesses were established by their current owners, and the proportion of Korean enclave business owners who bought established businesses is marginal.

Therefore, Korean entrepreneurship in Atlanta offers advantages in the ethnic economy, which are slightly different from those available in other cities. That is, the knowledge that Korean immigrants have access to two economic niches in the enclave in the Korean community and non-enclave in the inner city neighborhoods and in middle class neighborhoods, assist them to operate their own businesses in either economic niches. Korean entrepreneurs in Atlanta tend to be pioneers who expanded and established businesses on their own based on the models of economic structures developed in other cities, instead of fitting into already established businesses.

In the earlier chapter, RCA was not such an important capital resource for business establishment. However, quite a large proportion of Korean entrepreneurs are involved in RCA. Despite rare usage of RCA for business establishment, the RCA is very much oriented toward business operation rather than establishment. That is, capital mobilized in RCA is utilized for the maintenance of businesses more often through further investment and finance for the current businesses.

As a result, unlike other studies that generally predict ethnic resources are crucial for immigrant entrepreneurship, ethnic resources are more crucial after businesses are established. On the contrary, there is no indication of the importance of ethnic resources for business establishment other than ecological succession, which was not such a strong factor in the Atlanta Korean community because of a short history. Therefore, to contemplate ethnic entrepreneurship throughly, we need to investigate contributing factors more specifically, so that we can find out which resources are useful at which stages.

ETHNIC RESOURCES IN ETHNIC EMPLOYEES

A labor supply of ethnic employees is another advantage for Korean entrepreneurs. Table 7-4 shows the traits of labor in Korean businesses in the enclave and non-enclave economies. Researchers found two sources of labor supply—unpaid family labor and cheap coethnic labor (Portes and Manning, 1986; Portes and Jensen, 1989; Waldinger et al., 1985). As discussed earlier, unpaid family labor is crucial for a large portion of Korean businesses. In addition, the coethnic labor force is also advantageous for ethnic entrepreneurs, because coethnic laborers generally have a commitment to work hard and long hours.

Although the utilization of coethnic labor is not a determinant for the formation of economic niches, they are resources that allow immigrant entrepreneurs to become competitive in their economic niches and that enable them to survive despite a lack of resources. As one can expect, Korean entrepreneurs, in general, heavily rely on Korean employees as a source of labor. Businesses in the enclave economy tend to exclusively rely on coethnic employees with some Hispanic employees, whereas the non-enclave economy not only relys on Korean employees, but also heavily relys on other ethnic groups such as African-American.

Unlike expectations that coethnic employees provide a source of cheap labor, entrepreneurs do not seem to perceive Korean employees as cheap labor, but rather that coethnic labor is more utilized for service in the enclave and trust in the non-enclave. As an interviewee in the non-enclave economy explained about coethnic labor:

In fact, Korean employees are more expensive than the local community people. Despite the higher labor price, the advantages of

Table 7-4: Ethnic Resources in Ethnic Employees (%)

	Enclave businesses	Non-enclave businesses	Total
Total number of interviewees (N)	70	89	159
Businesses with employees (N)	46	73	119
Ethnicity of employees			
Koreans	89.1	72.6	79.0
Blacks	2.2	56.2	35.3
Whites	17.4	26.0	22.7
Hispanics	26.1	17.8	21.0
Proportion of Korean employees among all employees	65.4	48.1	56.8
Reason to hire Korean employees			
Better communication	31.7	20.8	25.5
Hard worker	26.8	41.5	35.1
Trustworthy	12.2	60.4	39.4
Personal relations	12.2	18.9	16.0
Korean customers	70.7	3.8	33.0
Reason to hire African-American employees			
Good relationship with communities	0.0	61.0	59.5
Hard worker	0.0	9.8	9.5
Low wages	0.0	22.0	21.4
Availability	0.0	7.3	7.1
English skills			
Excellent	5.7	1.1	3.1
Good	17.1	14.6	15.7
Fair	48.6	50.6	49.7
Poor	12.9	27.0	20.8
Very poor	15.7	6.7	10.7
English is barrier for business operations	45.7	55.1	50.9

Korean employees are that I can ask them to work as hard as and sometimes as long as I do. Since the employee wants to open his own business in the future, he works hard with me. Although I cannot ask

American employees to work after the store is closed, I can do it to Koreans. If I have stocks coming in after the store hours, I cannot organize and shelve all the merchandise alone. So, I ask Korean employees to stay to finish shelving the merchandise. Although it is rare, when I am not present I can let the employees take over the cashier's counter and also I can ask to manage the store. Most of the time, either I or my wife is here to manage the store.

The reasons for hiring Korean employees are largely different on the basis of the economic niches. Entrepreneurs in the enclave economy hire Korean employees for quite a simple reason; as one put it, "all the customers are Koreans and it is natural Korean employees will serve Korean customers better." On the other hand, a large proportion of entrepreneurs in the non-enclave hire Koreans for trust and hard work. That is, although the proportion of Korean employees among all employees is much lower in the non-enclave, entrepreneurs in the non-enclave tend to hire Korean employees to manage the store or supervise other ethnic employees. Consequently, most entrepreneurs in the non-enclave hire Korean employees only for a specific position that is related with cash. However, due to the limited information on this issue, it is hard to determine whether the attitude of Korean merchants in the non-enclave economy is induced by discrimination against blacks or whether it is induced by familiarity with Korean immigrant workers.

With regard to their reason to hire African-American employees, other than the manger positions, entrepreneurs in the non-enclave hire local community people to avoid potential antagonism toward Korean merchants or because they have easier access to African-American employees for a cheap price. As a result, the Korean businesses that hire African-American employees are only in the non-enclave, most often they are businesses in the inner city neighborhoods. An entrepreneur in the non-enclave who tries to avoid conflict with the community members said as follows:

> I have mostly black customers. We know that blacks claim that Korean entrepreneurs exploit assets in their community, without returning profits to the community. So, our response to that claim is to give them job opportunities. It is also beneficial to have black employees, especially when arguments arise with black customers. Although customers would not listen to or believe me, they usually listen to black employees.

Large businesses in the non-enclave seem to have a rather ordinary reason to employ black labor. That is, African-American employees are easy to find and cheap to hire. As one interviewee who owns a grocery store as large as a franchise store said:

> My business is in the black residential area. It is easier to hire black employees than any other race, because I receive people looking for jobs almost everyday. Their labor price is also cheap. I have only a few Korean employees and I let them manage the store. All others are black employees, shelving stocks or cash registering. My wife is the top manager at the store.

Therefore, entrepreneurs in the non-enclave economy seem to receive a greater advantage from cheap labor than those in the enclave. That is, whereas those in the enclave need to hire Korean labor despite the higher cost, those in the non-enclave have more choice in their source of cheap labor from local people.

As a result, Korean entrepreneurs in the enclave hire Hispanics because of the lower labor cost, avoiding the higher labor cost of Korean employees. Entrepreneurs also hire Hispanic employees because they are good workers, citing them as "diligent and hard-working." Although the proportion of Hispanic employees hired in the non-enclave businesses is not sufficiently significant to cause conflict with the local community in Atlanta, Min (1996) found in New York that a dramatic increase in the rate of Hispanic employees in Korean businesses in the black community caused a notable conflict between Korean merchants and the local community.

Although English skills of entrepreneurs are not a part of ethnic resources, the skills are examined here since they are a factor in that they force immigrants to pursue entrepreneurship due to disadvantages in the labor market caused by insufficient language skills (Waldinger, 1989; Light, 1984). However, English skills do not seem to influence which economic niches Korean immigrants occupy. Korean entrepreneurs both in the enclave and non-enclave economy are not quite confident in their English skills, a large proportion of them responding that their English is "just fair." Considering that the English skills do not vary much between entrepreneurs in the enclave and non-enclave economies and that in fact, the language skill is slightly better among the enclave entrepreneurs, English skills do not seem to be fundamental in making a decision which economic niches they enter into.

However, limited English skills clearly cause entrepreneurs difficulties in operating businesses, which limit the development of businesses in the long run, and which prevent Korean entrepreneurs from getting into the larger economy in which business opportunities are more abundant. As an entrepreneur in the non-enclave said,

> I cannot communicate for the business matters very well. In fact, I do not need much English at this shop, either. It is a very simple procedure in that I just punch the cash register, when customers bring merchandise to the cashier's desk. Thus, conversations that I conduct at the business are very simple and limited. But the biggest problem is when I order products over the phone. It is especially hard to understand what the person on the other side of the phone line says. Another problem is when disputes with the customers arise. I cannot efficiently argue with customers because I cannot explain clearly in English.

However, they are also aware that their poor English causes misunderstanding with customers. Since the entrepreneurs in the non-enclave cannot have a chat with their customers due to the limited English skill, they often are misunderstood as if they are hostile against their customers. My personal experience during an interview with an entrepreneur in the non-enclave is that when I started conversation with a customer while he was paying, the customer became friendly with me and the store owner. After the customer left the store, the interviewee grumbled at her poor English, and said, "I wish I could speak like you. Then, I could easily make regular customers, because they would know that I am a friendly person." Therefore, their limited English skills not only cause misunderstanding, but also may hinder the growth of the business.

On the contrary, although English skills may not be crucial for business operation, entrepreneurs in the enclave economy rather strongly perceive poor language skills as one of the factors preventing them from opening businesses catering to non-Korean customers.

> I could not think of operating a business for American customers with my limited English skills. With my insufficient English, I would not be able to serve customers well and might go out of business. This

shop originally was owned by an American and I bought it from her. For the first time, I had quite a few American customers. But once they came in and found out that the owner changed to an Asian, they did not come anymore. It might be because of my English skills. Also, it could be that I am Asian and they do not want an Asian hairdresser. So, the majority of customers at my beauty shop have changed to Hispanics and Koreans.

Another interviewee who agreed that insufficient English skills caused a limitation in selecting business types said,

Because I have a language barrier and am unfamiliar with American culture, I could not start a business for American customers. Since I know what Korean customers are fond of, it is easier for me to start a business for Korean customers. Also, businesses for Koreans require less money than other businesses for black customers and these types of business do not require much skill, either. Because the Korean market is limited, I would like to expand customers from Koreans to other minority groups or white Americans.

Although some entrepreneurs in the enclave economy consider their English skills problematic for opening a business in the non-enclave economy, the fact that a high proportion of entrepreneurs with lower English skills operate businesses catering to non-Korean customers proves that English skills are not a decisive factor for getting into the non-enclave economy. However, English skills may prevent Korean immigrants from getting into the larger economy.

SUMMARY

This chapter examined factors affecting the division of Korean businesses into the enclave and the non-enclave niches. Since enclave and network theories (Waldinger et al., 1990; Portes and Manning, 1986; Aldrich and Zimmer, 1986) deal only with one factor at a time, the theories have limited capacity for explaining the dynamics of immigrant entrepreneurship and how immigrant economic structures are formed. Therefore, to contemplate the formation of immigrant entrepreneurial economic niches, it is necessary to examine how these factors interact to develop two economic structures in the immigrant community.

Korean immigrants have both advantages and disadvantages in business establishment. The disadvantage is that there are only two economic niches available to operate small businesses: one in the enclave economy for Korean customers and the other in the non-enclave eocnomy for inner city neighborhoods and a few middle class neighborhoods. The advantage is that Korean immigrants have sources to mobilize resources. This study indicates that immigrants who mibilize information through social networks tend to enter non-enclave businesses. In addition, since the capital requirement to open non-enclave businesses is considerably higher than that in the enclave economy, those who are capable of mobilizing large business capital through family networks or bank loans also tend to enter the non-enclave businesses. Therefore, although two economic niches are available in the enclave and the non-enclave, an immigrant's capacity to establish social networks and/or to mobilize larger capital further influences opportunities to open businesses in the non-enclave economy, the economic niche with higher economic returns. As a result, opportunities to get into the non-enclave economy are a result of an individual capacity to mobilize resources through social and family networks.

Ethnic resources do not seem to influence the occupancy of either economic niches. However, unlike the widely accepted belief that ethnic resources help immigrants enter entrepreneurship, ethnic resources are crucial for Korean immigrant entrepreneurs only after a business is established and rather useless before business establishment. However, despite that small businesses are risky and not very stable, ethnic resources furnish immigrant entrepreneurs with competitiveness by exploiting themselves and family members. As shown in Table 7-4, although Korean coethnic labor is no longer a source of cheap labor for Korean entrepreneurs, it provides a reliable source of labor which allows business owners to take care of other more productive tasks rather than manual labor. Thus, ethnic resources have a fundamental importance for competitiveness for immigrant entrepreneurs.

Although the chances are rare, a few found opportunities for catering to middle class neighborhoods. The opportunities are also influenced by both factors of economic niches and individual capacity to mobilize business information through social networks and capital through family networks or other sources. Considering the existence of opportunities in sectors other than the enclave in the Korean community and non-enclave in the inner city neighborhoods, the issue of whether Korean immigrants will move further up the ladder of the economic hierarchy depends upon how Korean immigrants capitalize such opportunities in the mainstream economy.

CHAPTER VIII
Conclusion

Despite arguments that self-employment is an obsolete aspect of the capitalist economic system (O'Connor, 1973: Ch 1; Horvat, 1982: Ch 1), Korean immigrants in the United States, like many other immigrants, have displayed a high propensity for entrepreneurship, with one of the highest rates of entrepreneurship among the recent immigrants since the 1965 Immigration Amendment Act. Given that the Korean-American community in Atlanta has recently undergone dramatic growth and there is a high rate of entrepreneurship among this group, this study offers an opportunity to study entrepreneurial pursuit of Korean immigrants by utilizing networks, class resources and ethnic resources. This study has focused on five major issues concerning: (1) the relationships between networks and class resources as determined by educational background; (2) the distinctions between social networks and family networks; (3) the utilization of social networks and family networks for business establishment by Korean immigrants; (4) the factors that split Korean entrepreneurs into two economic niches, inside the enclave and outside it; (5) the utilization of ethnic resources for Korean business entrepreneurship.

FINDINGS

As to the first issue, this study found that there is an indispensable interconnection between class resources and the establishment of social networks. Researchers (Bates, 1994a, 1997; Sanders and Nee, 1996) found that class resources, represented by educational level, constitute a valuable resource for immigrants who seek to become entrepreneurs. In addition, Yoon (1991c) argues that class resources are crucial as businesses grow and enter an advanced stage. Although these previous investigations have found that class resources are important, they do not show how class resources are capitalized to help the establishment of businesses. However, this study found that those with a higher educational background establish social networks from a larger variety of sources, and that the social networks are crucial for resource mobilization. As a result, those with a higher educational background start businesses in a shorter period or immediately after immigration. In addition, social networks established on the basis of educational background are the major sources of business information for business operation. Therefore, social networks and class resources have a fundamental connection and are crucial resources for business establishment not just in early stage but in every stage of business development.

As to the second and third issues, social networks and family networks have a clear distinction in the way they generate resources for business establishment. Although numerous studies have dealt with network utilization by immigrant entrepreneurs (Aldrich and Zimmer, 1986; Zimmer and Aldrich, 1987; Goldberg, 1985), they vaguely conclude that networks are crucial for immigrant entrepreneurship without precise evidence as to how networks are established, how networks are utilized for business formation, or how different networks generate different resources to facilitate immigrant entrepreneurship. As a consequence, in this study, networks are divided into two components: family networks and social networks. This division makes it clear that family networks and social networks operate distinctively and generate different resources: family networks for business capital; social networks for business information.

Sanders and Nee (1996) argue based on Census data that family (e.g., spouse, in-laws, and relatives) should be considered a form of social capital, as it provides mutual obligation, trust, and cooperative group efforts, which enhance the probability of establishing businesses. However, since they do not distinguish between family networks and social networks, they come to a vague conclusion that it is not clear how social capital helps a group establish businesses. Therefore, social networks and family networks must be considered separately to examine specific types of resources that are generated through the networks (i.e., social networks provide business information and family networks provide capital).

Social networks are mostly established through involvement in church, associations, or organizations in the community. These organizational settings are crucial for Korean entrepreneurship, because they provide Korean immigrants with a venue to establish social networks which are fundamental for generating resources for business establishment. Although churches are meant for religious gatherings, and other associations such as alumni and Korean community associations are meant for social gatherings, Korean immigrants participate in them to "keep in touch" with other community members for access and updates to business information, and to expand customers for their enclave businesses.

Therefore, it is not just business associations that generate resources necessary for businesses; all other associations, organizations, and even churches are places where Korean immigrants have access to business resources. Therefore, social networks are the most crucial source from which Koreans gain information about business opportunities either in the enclave or outside it. In addition, social networks and family networks operate differently and lead Korean immigrants into different economic paths. Those who have obtained business information from social networks tend to enter the economic niche outside the enclave, where economic returns are higher.

Furthermore, those with a higher educational background seem to make better use of existing resources (e.g., money brought from Korea) for their business establishments. Since those with higher levels of education tend to have prompt access to established social networks, and most business information is acquired through these networks, social networks enable those with higher class resources to start businesses quicker and utilize their resources more efficiently.

Immigrants with family networks have been perceived to have the advantage of information about job opportunities and future entrepreneurial possibilities (Massey et al., 1987; Massey, 1988; Tilly, 1990; Taylor, 1986; White, 1970), and family networks are thought to provide fundamental resources for immigrant business establishment (Senders and Nee, 1996; Werbner, 1987). Contrary to the perceptions, chain-migrants in Atlanta are not able to start their own businesses more quickly than non-chain migrants. In addition, although chain-migrants might have some advantages in getting jobs in order to make a living after immigration, family networks do not seem to provide access to prestigious jobs, and like other immigrants they are limited to low-wage, low-skill, low-prestige jobs. However, this analysis finds that it is social networks facilitated by educational background that enables Korean immigrants to start businesses more quickly and enter the economic niche with higher returns.

However, independent of their possession of family networks, recent Korean immigrants usually came with the intention of operating businesses. As a result, immigrants came since the 1980s tend to be employed in the enclave economy to a greater extent than the earlier immigrants. Eventually, this employment experience in the enclave economy can be viewed as a social networks, since Korean immigrants who work in the enclave economy gain the information and skills necessary to run their businesses.

As to the fourth issues, the source of information mobilization and the capacity for larger business capital mobilization lead Korean entrepreneurs into different economic niches. A much higher proportion of those who obtained business information through social networks went into businesses in the non-enclave economy, which has higher economic rewards. Therefore, information generated by social networks provides useful resources to start businesses, as well as better prospects in business. In contrast, a significant proportion of the Korean entrepreneurs in the enclave have relied more on personal resources (e.g., skills brought from Korea) than information gathered from social networks.

The most common source of capital is personal savings. In addition, regardless of whether they are chain-migrants, many Korean immigrants rely on family networks for business capital loans. Unexpectedly, a significant proportion of Korean entrepreneurs with prior business experience obtained loans from banks. Even though utilization of family and social networks for business capital provision does not vary much according to the economic niche, obtaining bank loans is higher among entrepreneurs outside the enclave economy. Since businesses outside the enclave require more start-up capital, personal loans from family or friends are inadequate. Since non-enclave entrepreneurs are also more likely to have had prior business experiences, prior experience also enables them to acquire loans from banks based on their credit histories, which enable them into non-enclave businesses. That suggests that as Korean immigrants live in the U.S. longer and acquire credit histories by running businesses, they are not solely dependent on capital resources generated within the ethnic community. They can instead turn to the mainstream society.

English skills do not seem to be especially crucial for getting into businesses at the beginning, nor for getting into the non-enclave economic niche. In fact, although entrepreneurs catering to American customers worry about their English skills and think that better English skills will help their businesses, English skills do not seem to be crucial when starting. However, with limited language skills, they are very well aware of a limit to the types of business they can operate. In other words, with a limited capacity for communication, Korean entrepreneurs will not be able to leap into a larger economy by catering to the general population.

As to the fifth issue, ethnic resources are crucial resources for immigrant entrepreneurship after businesses are established rather than during business establishment. A common belief has been that ethnic resources make Asian immigrants more prone to be entrepreneurs and more likely to become successful (Kim and Hurh, 1985; Yoon, 1991c). In addition, note that both cultural theory and enclave theory (Light, 1980, 1984; Light and Bonacich, 1988; Werbner, 1984; Portes and Manning, 1986) argue that utilization of ethnic resources (e.g., RCA: Kye, hard work, unpaid family labor, and cheap coethnic labor) is essential for business establishment. However, this study shows that these ethnic resources are not such crucial elements for business establishment, but are more useful after businesses are established. Therefore, after businesses are established, the ethnic resources give a competitive advantage over other ethnic or minority groups who do not utilize or have such resources.

As the high proportion of Korean entrepreneurs involved in rotating credit associations reveals, many entrepreneurs make use of the money collected through RCA for the current business investments. Many researchers (Geertz, 1962; Light, 1972; Light et al., 1990; I. Kim, 1981) argue RCA, that is unique and wide spread ethnic resources among many Asian immigrants, provides business capital, which explains why Asian immigrants are so likely to become entrepreneurs. However, an understanding of the effect of RCA should consider how they are used by immigrant entrepreneurs. That is, although only a small proportion of Korean entrepreneurs in Atlanta have utilized RCA for start-up capital, a large proportion of them utilized RCA for further investments for the current businesses.

Therefore, although RCA is not utilized extensively for the establishment of business, it is crucial resource widely utilized for maintenance and further investment such as buying stock to shelve. As a result, RCA provide a competitive advantage that enables Korean entrepreneurs to stay in business and possibly reduce turnover rate compared with other ethnic businesses. In addition, although money brought from Korea has been recognized as an important source of business capital (Min, 1996), it has only been those who immigrated since the 1980s who have relied on this source. Further, among those who brought money from Korea, the capital was generally not enough for a business establishment and they needed to borrow additional money from family or friends.

Unlike the argument of enclave theory, Korean entrepreneurs no longer have the advantage of cheap Korean labor, because Korean immigrant labor is actually more expensive than other minority labor. The high price of Korean immigrant labor has made entrepreneurs turn to other minorities (e.g., Hispanics). Although Korean entrepreneurs hire cheap labor from other ethnic groups and hire only a small number of Korean employees, they tend to hire Korean employees for managerial positions, especially in non-enclave businesses. This tendency is because Korean entrepreneurs have more trust in coethnic laborers. Businesses in the non-enclave economy utilize unpaid family labor more often and consider it more important for business operation than their counterparts. In addition, the value of unpaid family labor becomes more significant when the size of the business becomes larger. However, unpaid family labor has little to do with business creation.

In addition, this study found that, as business information mobilized from social networks influence the decision of which economic niches to occupy, structural opportunities are closely tied to the resources that are available based on an individual's social networks. As a result, taking these factors (i.e., structural opportunity and social networks) separately, do not provide a full picture of Korean entrepreneurship. Consequently, by contemplating advantages and disadvantages on a personal level (i.e., social and family networks, ethnic resources, and class resources) as well as on a structural level (i.e., enclave and non-enclave economy) simultaneously, this study has examined not only how Korean immigrants get into entrepreneurship, but also how they manage those businesses by utilizing their ethnic resources.

FURTHER RESEARCH AGENDA

Several issues call for attention in further research. There have been many studies of immigrant entrepreneurship, including some of Korean immigrants. There has also been much debate concerning the factors that influence certain immigrant groups to demonstrate a propensity for entrepreneurship. However, there has been little study of what the consequences of ethnic businesses are. In other words, are ethnic businesses really helpful for the economic mobility of ethnic groups; what are the effects of ethnic business on family life such as gender roles and attitudes; and will second-generation Korean-Americans follow the steps of their parents in small businesses?

Since a large portion of Korean entrepreneurship is located in the peripheral economy catering to the lower strata of the American population, Korean immigrants work very hard for low economic rewards. Although a large proportion of Korean immigrants have successfully moved away from marginal occupations by establishing businesses, it is questionable whether the business operations provide real economic and social mobility for Korean immigrants, considering their work environments and economic rewards. In addition, if entrepreneurship is truly the only path that disadvantaged minorities can follow to get ahead, it will be valuable to find out whether the ways Korean immigrants take to become entrepreneurs are applicable to other disadvantaged ethnic groups, minorities, or women.

Also, there are concerns about Korean immigrant families. Since both parents work from dawn to night at businesses, many families are faced with difficulties in the education of their children. The education of children includes not only school education, but also education for cultural values. Due to the traditional emphasis on higher education, the educational level of Korean children is higher than that of other ethnic groups. However, as their children grow up to be members of the mainstream society, the Korean immigrant parents encounter a cultural gap with their children in that they find it hard to communicate with them, both because of English skills and different cultural orientations. In addition, there has been a drastic change in gender roles in the Korean family, as both wife and husband typically work. One of the recognizable changes is an increased independence of wives. Since these changes have an impact on Korean-American families, the changes merit attention for further ethnic studies on Korean immigrants.

In addition, there are issues related to second generation Korean-Americans and teenage migrants. Although my data include teenage migrants, they were not studied extensively enough to draw significant conclusions. There are questions as to how much the second-generation and 1.5 generation attach themselves to Korean ethnic identities, as well as how successfully they blend into the mainstream society. Since Asian immigrants are in a different situation than European immigrants who have successfully melted into the pot of the mainstream society, the second generation of Asian immigrants merits attention to see how they identify themselves.

With regard to ethnic entrepreneurship, first, there need to be other studies to determine whether the findings in this study are generalizable. There is a problem of generalization due to the homogeneous sample collected only in the Korean community in Atlanta. The lack of samples from other ethnic groups for comparison limits the generalization of these findings. Once tendencies are generalizable, there can be policy implementations to help those disadvantaged minorities.

Second, the consequences of Korean immigrants' commercial activities in African-American neighborhoods should be further studied, since a large proportion of Korean businesses are located near African-American neighborhoods, and the neighbors are antagonistic to Korean merchants. Although there have been studies done after the Los Angeles riots that suggest that the hostility is induced by a mutual misunderstanding of cultures, more studies should be done for a better understanding between the groups to reduce further conflicts and animosity.

APPENDIX
Interview Schedule

INTERVIEW SCHEDULE

JIN-KYUNG YOO

**DEPARTMENT OF SOCIOLOGY
UNIVERSITY OF GEORGIA**

The study of immigrant entrepreneurship has drawn much attention in the sociological fields due to a large impact on immigrants' socioeconomic status in the United States. Since the studies in the immigrant entrepreneurship that have been done so far are somewhat limited for full incitement of inner characteristics, I am conducting the survey to find out which explanations might have been left out in the study of immigrant entrepreneurship. The questionnaire will take about 40 minutes to answer. I appreciate for your cooperation and time.

1.   When did you start your current business?   _____

                                                       month/year

2.   What is the type of current business?

           Specify _____

3.   What is the motivation to start the current type of business(es)?

4.   What was the source of information?

5.   Who are the major customers of your store?

          Race: _____ (%)

                   _____ (%)

                   _____ (%)

      5a.   Do you have any reason why you made a decision of serving Koreans

                (or Blacks) for your business?

      If you have Korean customers, do you offer special services or benefits to

      Korean customers?

             Yes   (   )   No   (   )

      If yes, what kind of benefits are they?

6.   Why do you think a certain race of customers became a major customers of your store?

      (1)   Because of the location of the store (closeness)

      (2)   Because of products my store carry

      (3)   Because of special services or benefits to customers offered in the store

      (4)   Because of their poor English language skill

      (5)   Others, specify   _____

7.   Why did you locate your store at the current place?

     (1)   _____

     (2)   _____

     (3)   _____

     7a.   Have you thought of locating businesses in other locations: for example, serving other ethnic groups or better locations?

     7b.   If you did, why and where?

8.   Do you currently own more store(s) in addition to the present store?

         Yes ( )   No ( )

     If yes, how many?   _____

        What is the type(s) of business(es)?

             Specify _____

        Why did you choose the type(s) of business(es)?

             Specify _____

        Who is in charge with the other business(es)?

             Specify _____

9.   What is the annual gross sale (before taxes) of your store?

     (1) Under $30,000   (2) $30,000 - $49,999

     (3) $50,000 - $99,999   (4) $100,000 - $299,999

     (5) $300,000 - $499,999   (6) $500,000 - $999,999

     (7) $1,000,000 or more

10. How did you capitalize your current business?

(Choose three the most important financial resources and rank them in order.)

Loan from friends .... ( )

Loan from family members or relatives .... ( )

Loan from bank(s) .... ( )

Money brought from Korea .... ( )

Partnership .... ( )

Own savings .... ( )

Credit rotating association .... ( )

Loan from Small Business Association .... ( )

10a. How much did you pay for the current business?

11. Have you ever participated in a credit rotating association before?

Yes ( )   No ( )==> go to no. 15.

If yes, on average how many members were in a credit rotating association?

If yes, what was your relationship with the members?

(1) Friends   (2) Businessmen

(3) Alumni   (4) Relatives

(5) Church members Other _____

12. Was credit rotating association useful to capitalize your business?

(1) very useful

(2) more or less useful

(3) more or less **not** useful

(4) not useful at all

13. Why did you participate in a credit rotating association?

To capitalize the first business .... ( )

Friendship and social meeting .... ( )

Savings .... ( )

To finance on-going business .... ( )

To buy a house, a car or other .... ( )

To finance some ceremony .... ( )

such as a funeral or a wedding .... ( )

14. Do you think that credit rotating association is useful for Korean businessmen in the U.S. for economic or social (e.g., social meeting) purposes?

	Yes	No	Don't Know
Economic:	( )	( )	( )
Social:	( )	( )	( )

15. Did you bring any money from Korea at the time of immigration?

Yes ( ) No ( )==> go to no. 16.

15a. How much did you bring?

15b. Was money brought from Korea important to capitalize your first business?

(1) very important

(2) more or less important

(3) more or less **not** important

(4) not important at all

16.   Do you have any paid employee(s) in your store?

Yes   (   )   No   (   )

If yes, please provide the following information?

Ethnicity	Number	Full-time worker	Part-time worker	Wage per hour

17.   If you have Korean employee(s), are there special reasons to prefer Korean to non-Koreans? (Choose two the most important reasons)

(1) Better communication with Korean employees

(2) Because they work harder and better

(3) Trustworthy

(4) Low wage

(5) Personal relationship or recommendation from others

(6) Because major customers are Koreans

18.   Are there any disadvantages in hiring Korean employees? If so, what are they?

(1) _____

(2) _____

(3) _____

19.   Do you have non-Korean employee(s)?

      Yes   (   )   No   (   )

      19a.   **If yes**, are there special reasons for hiring them?

      (1) Because major customers are non-Koreans (i.e., blacks or Hispanics)

      (2) Low wage

      (3) To have better relationship with local community

      (4) Other, specify _____

20.   How did you find your current employee(s)? (Choose as many as applicable)

      (1) Advertisement on Korean newspaper

      (2) Personal relationship (e.g., family members or relatives)

      (3) Recommendation from others

      (4) They visited the store

      (5) They were employees of the previous owner

      Other, specify _____

21.   Are you personally related with your Korean employee(s) (i.e., friends or family)?

      Yes   (   )   No   (   )

      If yes, what is the relationship?

22. Do you think that your Korean employees are planning to open their own businesses in the future?

    Yes   (   )   No   (   )

    If yes, how do they plan to capitalize for their future businesses?

    (1) Personal saving

    (2) Loan from banks

    (3) Loan from friends

    (4) Loan from family members or relatives

    (5) Credit rotating association

    (6) Other, specify _____

23. Please provide the information about family member(s) (unpaid labor) who work in your store?

Relationship with respondent	Age	Type of work	Working hours per week

24. Do you think that help from family members is important for the success of your business?

    (1) Very important

    (2) More or less important

    (3) More or less **not** important

    (4) Not important at all

25. What is the working hours of your store?

(1) Weekdays:

(2) Saturdays:

(3) Sundays:

26. How long do your actually work in your store?

(1) Weekdays:

(2) Saturdays:

(3) Sundays:

27. Who supervises your store when you are absent?

28. Have you ever engaged in a self-employment in Korea before you immigrate to the United States?

Yes   (   )   No   (   )

If yes, what was the type of business?

If yes, how long have you engaged in it?

If no, what was your occupation in Korean (Please specify your company and your position at the company, and your income per month)?

Company ───────────────────────────────

Position ───────────────────────────────

Income ───────────────────────────────
(per month)

29. Have you engaged any other businesses in the U.S. other than the
current one?

      Yes (   )   No   (   )

If yes, was it:

    (1) Minority-oriented

    (2) Korean-oriented

    (3) Other (please specify) _____

If yes, please provide the following information about the prior business(es).

	Type	Duration	Location	Ethnicity and # of employee(s)	Income
1st					
2nd					
3rd					
4th					

30. **If yes**, how did you capitalize the business(es)?

(Choose three the most important financial resources and rank them in order.)

    Loan from friends .... (   )

    Loan from family members or relatives .... (   )

    Loan from bank(s) .... (   )

    Money brought from Korea .... (   )

    Partnership .... (   )

    Own savings .... (   )

    Credit rotating association .... (   )

    Loan from Small Business Association .... (   )

31. Have you ever worked at Korean-owned shops or American-owned businesses?

    Yes ( ) No ( )

    If yes, please provide the following information.

Type	Duration	Location	Ethnicity of employer	Wage

32. Have you ever thought of getting a job equivalent to your educational level in America?

    Yes ( )===> go to No. 33 No ( )===> go to No. 34

33. Did you get a job?

    Yes ( ) No ( )

    If yes, what kind?

    If no, why?

34. Why did you decide against other types of work other than self-employment?

35. How long did it take until you open your own business after you made decision to engage in small business of your own? _____

36. Did you buy out an already established store?

    Yes ( ) No ( ) ===> skip to no. 40.

37. What was the ethnicity of the previous owner?

38. How did you find the previous owner?
    (1) Advertisement
    (2) Real estate agency
    (3) Recommendation from others
    (4) Personal relationship (e.g., family members, relatives or acquaintance)
    (5) Other, specify ⎯⎯⎯⎯⎯⎯⎯⎯⎯⎯⎯⎯⎯⎯⎯

39. Why did you buy (or start) this business?

40. Do you seek the advise of anyone when you encounter problems or difficulties in managing your business? If so, who is that?

41. From whom do you receive help filling out tax forms, licenses, special permits and other types of governmental requirements for business?

42. Are you satisfied with your current business in term of the sales volume?
    (1) Very satisfied
    (2) More or less satisfied
    (3) More or less **not** satisfied
    (4) very dissatisfied

43. Did you expand your business after you opened it up?

    (1) Substantially expanded

    (2) Somewhat expanded

    (3) Same

    (4) Smaller

44. Do you plan to expand more in the future?

        Yes (   )   No (   )

    If yes, do you plan to expand in the current location or move to another location: for example, looking for other types of customers?

    Why do you **move** to other location or **keep** the location?

45. What are the problems or difficulties in managing your business?

    (1) _____

    (2) _____

    (3) _____

46. Do you think that your education, skills, earlier experience are being utilized in your business?

        Education: (1)   Utilized very much

                      (2)   Somewhat utilized

                      (3)   Not utilized very much

                      (4)   Not utilized at all

Skills: (1)   Utilized very much

(2)   Somewhat utilized

(3)   Not utilized very much

(4)   Not utilized at all

Earlier experience: (1)   Utilized very much

(2)   Somewhat utilized

(3)   Not utilized very much

(4)   Not utilized at all

47.   What factors do you think have motivated you to engage in small business in the United

State? (Choose three the most important factors and rank them)

(   )   Because I think that running a small business of one's own is one of the best ways
an immigrant can make a living, considering the fact of disadvantages of
immigrants in the labor market.

(   )   Because I liked to be my own boss.

(   )   Because I thought it was the best way for me to earn money.

(   )   Because I could not find a white collar job without pursing further education or
training.

(   )   Because I felt discriminated against in the labor market in terms of
promotion.

(   )   Because I felt business is better job than the one I could get in the labor
market.

(   )   If you have other reasons, please specify.

48.   What are your long-term business plan? For example, do you want to expand the current

business, buy another business, change location, or change type of business?

49. Do you think that you will inherit your business(s) to your children?

Yes ( )==> go to no. 50   No ( )

49a. Why not? _____

50. Do you currently attend any voluntary association(s) (e.g., church, social meeting, alumni meeting, or chamber of commerce etc.)?

Type & Purpose of association	Frequency of attendance	Position at the Association

If you are a member of any kinds of association(s) go to 50a, otherwise go to 50b.

50a. Do you get any benefits from the association(s)?

Yes ( )   No ( )

If yes, what kinds of benefits do you get?

If no, why do you think you don't get any benefits?

50b. What is the reason that you don't participate any associations?

51.   How do you evaluate your English language ability?

	Excellent	Good	Fair	Poor	Very poor
Listening:	( )	( )	( )	( )	( )
Speaking:	( )	( )	( )	( )	( )
Reading:	( )	( )	( )	( )	( )
Writing:	( )	( )	( )	( )	( )

52.   Do you speak English in your store?

(1)   Always

(2)   Often

(3)   Once in a while

(4)   Not at all

53.   Is English a barrier in managing your business?

Yes   (   )   No   (   )

If yes, whom do you turn to when you encounter language problems?

54.   Who are the primary competitors of your business?

Please provide the information about demographic characteristics of yourself and your family members.

55.   Your age: _____

Sex: _____

Place of residence in Korean (name of the city): _____

The year of immigration to the United States: _____

56.   If you have experience(s) of staying somewhere other than Atlanta in the U.S., please list the location(s) and describe how long you had been there (Otherwise, go to No. 57).

Location	Period	Occupation	Income

If you have experiences of living other cities, please explain why you have moved to Atlanta?

57.   Please list family members in the household.

Relationship with respondent	Age	Occupation

58.   How many years of schooling have you completed?

	in Korea	in the U.S.
Elementary school:	( )	( )
Middle school:	( )	( )
High school:	( )	( )
Vocational school:	( )	( )
College education but not finished:	( )	( )
College education:	( )	( )
Graduate education but not finished:	( )	( )
Graduate school:	( )	( )

If you have *college or vocational training*, what was your **major field of study**?

If you have *graduate education*, what was your **major field of study**?

59. What were the main reasons to come to the United States?

(Choose three major reasons and rank them in order.)

Economic opportunity	(	)
Own educational opportunity	(	)
Individual freedom	(	)
Educational opportunity for children	(	)
Aspiration for American way of life	(	)
Unification with family members in the U.S.	(	)
Social and political instability in Korea	(	)

Otner, specify ————————————————————

60. What was your father's occupation in Korea?

Thank you for your cooperation and time.

Bibliography

Aldrich, Howard. 1975. "Ecological Succession in Racially Changing Neighborhoods: A Review of the Literature." *Urban Affairs Quarterly* vol. 10. no. 3 (March): 327-348.

Aldrich, Howard and Albert J. Reiss, Jr. 1975. "Continuities in the Study of Ecological Succession: Changes in the Race Composition of Neighborhoods and Their Businesses." *American Journal of Sociology* vol. 81, no. 4: 846-866.

Aldrich, Howard and Catherine Zimmer. 1986. "Entrepreneurship through Social Networks." Pp. 3-23 in *The Art and Science of Entrepreneurship*, edited by Donald Sexton and Raymond Smilor. Cambridge, Mass: Ballinger Publishing Company.

Aldrich, Howard and Roger Waldinger. 1990. "Ethnicity and Entrepreneurship." *Annual Review of Sociology* vol. 16: 111-135.

Aldrich, Howard, Trevor Jones, and David McEvoy. 1984. "Ethnic Advantage and Minority Business Development." Ch. 11 in *Ethnic Communities in Business: Strategies for economic Survival*, edited by Robin Ward and Richard Jenkins. London/New York: Cambridge University Press.

Atlanta Regional Commission. 1995. *Ethnic Regional Community Profiles: Koreans in the Atlanta Region*. Atlanta: The Atlanta Regional Commission.

Bailey, Thomas and Roger Waldinger. 1991. "Primary, Secondary, and Enclave Labor Markets: A Training Systems Approach." *American Sociological Review* vol. 56 (August): 432-445.

Bates, Timothy. 1997. *Race, Self-employment, and Upward Mobility: An Illusive American Dream* Washington, D.C.: The Woodrow Wilson Center Press.

————. 1994a. "Social Resources Generated by Group Support Networks May Not Be Beneficial to Asian Immigrant-Owned Small Businesses." *Social Forces* vol. 72: 671-689.

————. 1994b. "An Analysis of Korean-Immigrant-Owned Small-Business Start-Ups with Comparisons to African-American and Nonminority-Owned firms." *Urban Affairs Quarterly* vol. 30, no. 2, December: 227-248.

Blalock, Hubert. 1967. *Toward a Theory of Minority-Group Relations* New York: John Wiley and Sons.

Bonacich, Edna. 1973. "A Theory of Middleman Minorities." *American Sociological Review* vol. 38 (October): 583-594.

————. 1984. "Some Basic Facts: Patterns of Asian Immigration and Exclusion." Pp. 277-315 in *Labor Immigration Under Capitalism: Asian Workers in the United States Before World War II*, edited by Lucie Cheng and Edna Bonacich. Los Angeles: University of California Press.

————. 1987. ""MAKING IT" in America: A Social Evaluation of the Ethics of Immigrant Entrepreneurship." *Sociological Perspectives* vol. 30, no. 4 (October): 446- 465.

Bonacich, Edna, Ivan Light, and Charles Choy Wong. 1976. "Small Business Among Koreans in Los Angeles." Pp.437-449 in *Counterpoint: Perspective on Asian America*, edited by Emma Gee. Los Angeles: Asian American Studies Center, University of California.

————. 1977. "Koreans in Business." *Society* vol. 14, no.6 (September-October): 54-59.

————. 1972. "A Theory of Ethnic Antagonism: The Split Labor Market." *American Sociological Review* 37(October):547-559.

Bonacich, Edna and John Modell. 1980. *The Economic Basis of Ethnic Solidarity: Small Business in the Japanese American Community* Berkeley: University of California Press.

Bonacich, Edna and Tae Hwan Jung. 1982. "A Portrait of Korean Small Business in Los Angeles." Pp. 75-98 in *Koreans in Los Angeles: Prospects and Promises*, edited by Eui-Yong Yu, Earl H. Phillips, and Eun-Sik Yang. Los Angeles: Koryo Research Institute, Center for Korean-American and Korean Studies, California State University.

Boyd, Monica. 1989. "Family and Personal Networks In International Migration: Recent Developments and New Agendas." *International Migration Review* vol. 23, No. 3: 638-670.

Brüderl, Josef and Peter Preisendörfer. 1997. "Network Support and the Success of Newly Founded Businesses." *Small Business Economics* vol. 9: 1-13.

Chinoy, Ely. 1952. "The Tradition of Opportunity and the Aspirations of Automobile Workers." *American Journal of Sociology* vol. 57: 453-459.

Chiswick, Barry. 1984. "Illegal Aliens in the United States Labor Market: Analysis of Occupational attainment and Earnings." *International Migration Review* vol. 18, no. 3: 714-732.

————. 1979. "The Economic Progress of Immigrants: Some Apparently Universal Patterns." Pp. 357-399 in *Contemporary Economic Problems*, edited by William Feller. Washington, D.C.: American Enterprise Institute.

Choy, Bong Youn. 1971. *Korea: A History*, forwarded by Younghill Kang. Rutland, VT.: C.E. Tuttle.

DeJong, Gordon F. and Robert W. Gardner. 1981 *Migration Decision Making: multidisciplinary approaches to micro level studies in developed and developing countries* New York: Pergamon.

Doeringer, Peter and Michael Piore. 1971. *Internal Labor Markets and Manpower Analysis* Lexington, Mass: Heath.

Southeast Newspaper Weekly (The). 1996. "Rethinking of the Past 10 Years of Korean Entrepreneurship in Atlanta." April

Fratoe, Frank A. 1986 "A Sociological Analysis of Minority Business." *Review of Black Political Economy* vol. 16: 33-50.

Geertz, Clifford. 1962. "The Rotating Credit Association: A 'Middle Rung' in Development." *Economic Development and Cultural Change* vol. 10 (April): 241-263.

Glazer, Nathan and Daniel Patrick Moynihan. 1963. *Beyond the Melting Pot: The Negroes, Puerto Ricans, Jews, Italians, and Irish of New York City* Cambridge: The MIT Press.

Goldberg, Michael A. 1985. *The Chinese Connection: Getting Plugged in to Pacific Rim Real Estate, Trade, and Capital Markets* Vancouver: University of British Columbia Press.

Goldscheider, Calvin and Frances Kobrin. 1980. "Ethnic Continuity and the Process of Self-Employment." *Ethnicity* vol. 7: 256-278.

Grieco, Margaret. 1987. "Family Networks and the Closure of Employment." Pp. 33- 44 in *The Manufacturing of Disadvantage*, edited by Gloria Lee and Ray Loveridge. Milton Keynes, England: Open University.

Hannerz, Ulf. 1974. " Ethnicity and Opportunity in Urban America." Pp. 37-76 in *Urban Ethnicity*, edited by Abner Cohen. London/New York: Tavistock Publications.

Hoffman, Constance A. and Martin N. Marger. 1991. "Patterns of Immigrant Enterprise in Six Metropolitan Areas." *Sociology and Social Research* vol. 75, no. 3 (April): 144-157.

Horvat, Branko. 1982. *The Political Economy of Socialism: A Marxist Social Theory* Armonk, NY: M.E. Sharpe.

Houchins, Lee and Chang-Su Houchins. 1974. "The Korean Experience in America, 1903-1924." *Pacific Historical Review* vol. 43, no. 4 (November): 548-575.

Hugo, Graeme J. 1981. "Village-Community Ties, Village Norms, and Ethnic and Social Networks: A Review of Evidence from the Third World." Pp. 186-224 in *Migration Decision-Making,* edited by Gordon F. DeJong and Robert W. Gardner. New York: Pergamon.

Hurh, Won Moo and Kwang Chung Kim. 1980. "Cultural and Social Adjustment Patterns of Korean Immigrants in the Chicago Area." Pp. 295-302 in *Sourcebook on the New Immigration: Implications for the United States and the International Community,* edited by Roy Simon Bryce-Laporte. New Brunswick, NJ: Transaction Books.

———. 1984. *Korean Immigrants in America: A Structural Analysis of Ethnic Confinement and Adhesive Adaptation* Rutherford/Madison/Teaneck: Fairleigh Dickinson University Press.

Jenkins, Richard. 1984. "Ethnic Minorities in business: A Research Agenda." Ch. 13 in *Ethnic Communities in Business: Strategies for economic Survival,* edited by Robin Ward and Richard Jenkins. London/New York: Cambridge University Press.

Kim, Bernice Bong Hee. 1934. "The Koreans in Hawaii." *Social Science* vol. 9, no. 4 (October): 409-413.

Kim, Hyung-Chan. 1974. "Some Aspects of Social Demography of Korean Americans." *International Migration Review* vol. 8, No. 1: 23-42.

Kim, Illsoo. 1981. *New Urban Immigrants: The Korean Community in New York* Princeton, NJ: Princeton University Press.

———. 1987. "The Koreans: Small Business in an Urban Frontier." Pp. 219-242 in *New Immigrants in New York,* edited by Nancy Foner. New York: Columbia University Press.

Kim, Kwang-Chung, and Won-Moo Hurh. 1985. "Ethnic Resources Utilization of Korean Immigrant Entrepreneurs in the Chicago Minority Area." *International Migration Review* vol. 19, no. 1: 82-111.

Kim, Kwang-Chung, Won-Moo Hurh, and Marilyn Fernandez. 1989. "Intra-Group Differences in Business Participation: Three Asian Immigrant Groups." *International Migration Review* vol. 23, no. 1: 73-95.

Kim, Won-Yong (Warren). 1971. *Koreans in America* Seoul: Po Chin Chai.

Light, Ivan. 1972. *Ethnic Enterprise in America: Business and Welfare Among Chinese, Japanese, and Blacks* Berkeley/Los Angeles: University of California Press.

————. 1979. "Disadvantage Minorities in Self-Employment." *International Journal of Comparative Sociology* vol. 20, no. 1-2: 31-45.

————. 1980. "Asian Enterprise in America: Chinese, Japanese, and Koreans in Small Business." Pp. 33-57 in *Self-Help in Urban America: Patterns of Minority Business Enterprise*, edited by Scott Cummings. Port Washington: Kennikat Press.

————. 1984. "Immigrant and Ethnic Enterprise in North America." *Ethnic and Racial Studies* vol. 7, no. 2 (April): 195-216).

————. 1985. "Immigrant Entrepreneurs in America: Koreans in Los Angeles." Pp. 161-178 in *Clamor at the Gates: The New American Immigration*, edited by Nathan Glazer. San Francisco: ICS Press, Institute for Contemporary Studies.

Light, Ivan and Edna Bonacich. 1988. *Immigrant Entrepreneurs: Koreans in Los Angeles 1965-1982* Los Angeles: University of California Press.

Light, Ivan, and Angel A. Sanchez. 1987. "Immigrant Entrepreneurs: In 272 SMSAs." Sociological Perspectives 30(4):373-399.

Light, Ivan, Georges Sabagh, Mehdi Bozorgmehr, and Claudia Der-Martirosian. 1993. "Internal Ethnictiy in the Ethnic Economy." *Ethnic and Racial Studies* vol. 16, no. 4: 581-597.

————. 1994. "Beyond the Ethnic Enclave Economy." *Social Problems* vol. 41, no. 1 (February): 65-80.

Light, Ivan, Im Jung Kwuon, and Deng Zhong. 1990. "Korean Rotating Credit Associations in Los Angeles." *Amerasia* vol. 16, no. 1: 35-54.

Light, Ivan, Parminder Bhachu, and Stavros Karageorgis. 1993. "Migration Networks and Immigrant Entrepreneurship." Pp. 25-50 in *Immigration and Entrepreneurship: Culture, Capital and Ethnic Networks*, edited by Ivan Light and Parminder Bhachu. New Brunswick, NJ: Transaction Publishers.

Light, Ivan and Stavros Karageorgis. 1994. "The Ethnic Economy." Pp. 648-671 in *The Handbook of conomic Sociology*, edited by Neil J. Smelser and Richard Swedberg. Princeton: Princeton University Press.

Lim, Lin Lean. 1987. "IUSSP Committee on International Migration, Workshop on International Migration Systems and Workshops." *International Migration Review* vol. 21, no. 2: 416-423.

Liu, John M. and Lucie Cheng. 1994. "Pacific Rim Development and the Duality of Post-1965 Asian Immigration to the United States." Pp. 74-99 in *The New Asian Immigration in Los Angeles and Global Restructuring*, edited by Paul Ong, Edna Bonacich, and Lucie Cheng. Philadelphia: Temple University Press.

Lomnitz, Larissa Adler. *Networks and Marginality: Lift in a Mexican Shantytown* Translated by Cinna Lomnitz. New York: Academic Press.

Mars, Gerald and Robin Ward. 1984. "Ethnic Business Development in Britain: Opportunities and Resources." Pp. 1-19 in *Ethnic Communities in Business: Strategies for Economic Survival*, edited by Robin Ward and Richard Jenkins. London/New York: Cambridge University Press.

Massey, Douglas S. 1988. "Economic Development and International Migration in Comparative Perspective." *Population and Development Review* vol. 14, no. 3, September: 383-413.

Massey, Douglas, Rafael Alarcon, Jorge Durand, and Humberto Gonzalez. 1987. *Return to Aztlan: The Social Process of International Migration from Western Mexico* Berkeley/Los Angeles: University of California Press.

Min, Pyong Gap. 1983. *Minority Business Enterprise: A Case Study of Korean Small Business in Atlanta* Ph.D. Dissertation: the Georgia State University.

————. 1987. "Factors Contributing to Ethnic Business: A Comprehensive Synthesis." *International Journal of Comparative Sociology* vol.28, no.3-4:173-193.

————. 1988. *Ethnic Business Enterprise: Korean Small Business in Atlanta* Island, NY: The Center for Migration Studies.

————. 1996. *Caught in the Middle: Korean Merchants in America's Multiethnic Cities* Los Angeles: University of California Press.

Modell, John. 1977. *The Economics and Politics of Racial Accommodation: The Japanese of Los Angeles* Urbana: University of Illinois Press.

Morawska, Ewa. 1989. "Labor Migrations of Poles in the Atlantic World Economy, 1880-1914." *Society for Comparative Study of Society and History* vol. 31: 237-272.

Morokvasic, Mirjana, Roger Waldinger, and Annie Phizacklea. 1990. "Business on the Ragged Edge: Immigrant and Minority Business in the Garment Industries of Paris, London, and New York." Pp. 157-176 in *Ethnic Entrepreneurs: Immigrant Business in Industrial Societies*, edited by Roger Waldinger, Howard Aldrich, Robin Ward, and Associates. Newbury Park/London/New Delhi: SAGE Publications.

North, David S. 1983. "Impact of Legal, Illegal, and Refugee Migrants on U.S. Social Service Programs." Pp. 269-286 in *Immigration and Refugee Policy: Global and Domestic Issues*, edited by Mary M. Kritz. Lexington, Mass.: Heath.

O'Connor, James. 1973. *The Fiscal Crisis of the State* New York: St. Martin's Press.

Office of the Federal Register National Archives and Records Administration (The). 1991. 8 Code of Federal Regulations, Part 214. Customs Duties. (56 FR 42952).

Ordino, Peter, Jr., M.C. 1968. "New Immigration Law in Retrospect." *International Migration Review* vol. 2, no. 3, Summer: 56-61.

Patterson, Wayne. 1977. "The first Attempt to Obtain Korean Laborers for Hawaii, 1896-1897." Pp.9-31 in *The Korean Diaspora: Historical and Sociological Studies of Korean Immigration and Assimilation in North America*, edited by Hyung-Chan Kim. Santa Barbara: ABC-Clio.

Pedraza, Silvia. 1994. "Introduction from the Special Issue Editor: The Sociology of Immigration, Race, and Ethnicity in America." *Social Problems* vol. 41, no. 1, February: 1-8.

Piore, Michael J. 1979. "Particular Characteristics of the migrant labor market." Ch. 4 in *Bird of Passage; Migrant Labor, and Industrial Societies* New York:: Cambridge University Press.

Pomerantz, Linda. 1984. "The Background of Korean Emigration." Pp.277-315 in *Labor Immigration Under Capitalism: Asian Workers in the United States Before World War II*, edited by Lucie Cheng and Edna Bonacich. Los Angeles: University of California Press.

Portes, Alejandro. 1978. "Migration and Underdevelopment." *Politics and Society* vol. 8, no. 1: 1-48.

———. 1979. "Illegal Immigration and the International System, Lessons from Recent Legal Mexican Immigrants to the United States." *Social Problems* vol. 26, no. 4, April: 425-437.

———. 1987. "The Social Origins of the Cuban Enclave Economy of Miami." *Sociological Perspectives* vol. 30, no. 4, October: 340-372.

———. 1995. "Economic Sociology and the Sociology of Immigration: A Conceptual Overview.' Pp. 1-41 in *The Economic Sociology of Immigration: Essays on Networks, Ethnicity, and Entrepreneurship*, edited by Alejandro Portes. New York: Russell Sage Foundation.

Portes, Alejandro, and Leif Jensen. 1989. "The Enclave and the Entrants: Patterns of Ethnic Enterprise in Miami Before and After Miriel." *American Sociological Review* vol. 54, no. 6, December: 929-949.

Portes, Alejandro, and Robert Manning. 1986. "The Immigrant Enclave: Theory and Empirical Examples." Pp. 47-68 in *Comparative Ethnic Relations*, edited by Susan Olzak and Joane Nagel. Orlando: Academic Press, Inc.

Rodino, Peter Jr., M.C. 1968. "New Immigration Law in Retrospect." *International Migration Review* vol. 2, no. 3 (Summer): 56-61.

Rose, Peter I. 1985. "Asian Americans: From Pariahs to Paragons." Pp. 181-212 in *Clamor at the Gates: the New American Immigration*, edited by Nathan Glazer. San Francisco: ICS Press.

Rubinson, Richard and Irene Browne. 1994. "Education and the Economy." Pp. 581-599 in *The Handbook of conomic Sociology*, edited by Neil J. Smelser and Richard Swedberg. Princeton: Princeton University Press.

Sanders, Jimy M. and Victor Nee. 1996. "Immigrant Self-Employment: The Family as Social Capital and the Value of Human Capital." *American Sociological Review* vol. 61 (April): 231-249.

Sassen-Koob, Saskia. 1980. "Immigrant and Minority Workers in the Organization of the Labor Process." *The Journal of Ethnic Studies* vol. 8, no. 1, Spring: 1-34.

Scase, Richard and Richard Goffee. 1987. *The Real World of the Small Business Owner* London: Croom Helm

———. 1982. *The Entrepreneurial Middle Class* London: Croom Helm.

Shapero, Albert, and Lisa Sokol. 1982. "The Social Dimensions of Entrepreneurship." Pp. 72-90 in *Encyclopedia of Entrepreneurship*, edited by Calvin A. Kent, Donald L. Sexton, and Karl H. Vesper. Englewood Cliffs, NY: Printice-Hall.

Taylor, Edward. 1986. "Differential Migration, Networks, Information and Risk." *Research in Human Capital and Development* vol. 4:147-71.

Tilly, Charles. 1990. "Transplanted Networks." Pp. 79-95 in *Migration Reconsidered: History, Sociology, and Politics*, edited by Virginia Yans-McLaughlin. New York: Oxford University Press.

Todaro, Michael P. 1976. *Internal Migration in Developing Countries: A Review of Theory, Evidence, Methodology, and Research Priorities* Geneva: International Labor Office.

Tsukashima, Ronald Tadao. 1991. "Cultural Endowment, Disadvantaged Status and Economic Niche: The Development of an Ethnic Trade." *International Migration Review* vol. 25, no. 2: 333-354.

Turner, Jonathan H. and Edna Bonacich. 1980. "Toward a Composite Theory of Middleman Minorities." *Ethnicity* vol. 7: 144-158.

U.S. Department of Commerce. Bureau of the Census. *Census of Population, General Population Characteristics, Metropolitan Areas* Washington, D.C.: GPO 1990.

U.S. Department of Commerce. Bureau of the Census. *Census of Population and Housing* Washington, D.C.: GPO 1910-1960.

U.S. Department of Commerce. Bureau of the Census. *Census of Population and Housing, Supplementary Reports about Metropolitan Areas* Washington, D.C.: GPO 1990.

U.S. Department of Commerce. Bureau of the Census. *Census of Population and Housing, Population and Housing characteristics for Census Tracts and Block Numbering Areas, Atlanta, GA MSA* Washington, D.C.: GPO 1990.

U.S. Department of Commerce. Bureau of the Census. *Census of Population and Housing, Population and Housing Characteristics for Census Tracts and Block Numbering Areas, Atlanta, GA MSA, Maps* Washington, D.C.: GPO 1990.

U.S. Department of Commerce. Bureau of the Census. *Census of Population: Social and Economic Characteristics, Georgia* Washington, D.C.: GPO 1990.

U.S. Department of Commerce. Bureau of the Census. *Economic Census, Survey of Minority-Owned Business Enterprises: Asian Americans, American Indians, and Other Minorities* Washington, D.C.: GPO 1992.

U.S. Department of Commerce. Bureau of the Census. *Economic Census, Survey of Minority-Owned Business Enterprises: Asian Americans, American Indians, and Other Minorities* Washington, D.C.: GPO 1987.

U.S. Department of Justice. Immigration and Naturalization Service. *Annual Reports: Immigration and Naturalization Service*, 1966-1977.

U.S. Department of Justice. Immigration and Naturalization Service. *Statistical Yearbook of the Immigration and Naturalization Service*, 1978-1993.

U.S. Department of Justice. Immigration and Naturalization Service. *Statistical Yearbook of the Immigration and Naturalization Service*, 1993. Appendix 1.

Waldinger, Roger. 1986. "Immigrant Enterprise: A Critique and Reformulation." *Theory and Society* vol. 15, no. 2: 249-285.

————. 1989. "Structural Opportunity or Ethnic Advantage? Immigrant Business Development in New York." *International Migration Review* vol. 23, no. 1: 48-72.

Waldinger, Roger and Howard Aldrich. 1990. "Trends in Ethnic Business in the United States." Pp. 49-78 in *Ethnic Entrepreneurs: Immigrant Business in Industrial Societies*, edited by Roger Waldinger, Howard Aldrich, Robin Ward, and Associates. Newbury Park/London/New Delhi: SAGE Publications.

Waldinger, Roger, Howard Aldrich, and Robin Ward. 1990. "Opportunities, Group Characteristics, and Strategies." Pp. 13-48 in *Ethnic Entrepreneurs: Immigrant Business in Industrial Societies*, edited by Roger Waldinger, Howard Aldrich, Robin Ward, and Associates. Newbury Park/London/New Delhi: SAGE Publications.

Waldinger, Roger, Robin Ward, and Howard Aldrich. 1985. "Ethnic Business and Occupational Mobility in Advanced Societies." *Sociology* vol. 19, no. 4 (November): 586-597.

Werbner, Pnina. 1984. "Business on trust: Pakistani Entrepreneurship in the Manchester Garment Trade." Pp.166-188 in *Ethnic Communities in Business: Strategies for Economic Survival,* edited by Robin Ward and Richard Jenkins. Cambridge, England: Cambridge University Press.

————. 1987. "13 Enclave Economies and Family Firms: Pakistani Traders in a British City." Pp.213-233 in *Migrants, Workers, and the Social Order,* edited by Jeremy Eades. London and New York: Tavistock Publications.

————. 1990a. "Chains of Entrepreneurs: The Production of an Enterprise Culture," Ch. 2 in *The Migration Process: Capital, Gifts and Offerings among British Pakistanis* New York: St. Martin's Press.

————. 1990b. "Renewing an Industrial Past: British Pakistani Entrepreneurship in Manchester." *Migration* vol. 8: 6-36.

Wilson, Kenneth L., and Alejandro Portes. 1980. "Immigrant Enclaves: An Analysis of the Labor Market Experiences of Cubans in Miami." *American Journal of Sociology* vol. 86, no. 2: 295-319.

Wilson, Kenneth L., and Allen Martin. 1982. "Ethnic Enclaves: A Comparison of the Cuban and Black Economies in Miami." *American Journal of Sociology* vol. 88, no. 1: 135-160.

White, Harrison. 1970. *Chains of Opportunity: System Models of Mobility in Organizations* Cambridge: Harvard University Press.

Yoo, Jin-Kyung. 1996. Dissertation. *Immigrant Entrepreneurs: Social & Family Networks and Ethnic Resources of Korean Immigrants in the Atlanta Metropolitan Statistical Area* The University of Georgia

Yoon, In-Jin. 1993. "The Social Origins of Korean Immigration to the United States from 1965 to the Present." *Papers of the Program on Population* No.121, September. Honolulu: East-West Center.

————. 1991a. "Immigrant Entrepreneurship: Korean Business in Chicago." Unpublished Paper Prepared for Presentation at the Race, Ethnicity and Urban Poverty Workshop, University of Chicago and Northwestern University.

————. 1991b. Dissertation. *Self-Employment in Business: Chinese-, Japanese-, and Korean-Americans, Blacks, and Whites* The University of Chicago

————. 1991c. "The Changing Significance of Ethnic and Class Resources in Immigrant Businesses: The Case of Korean Immigrant Businesses in Chicago." *International Migration Review* vol. 25, no. 2: 303-331.

Yu, Eui-Yong. 1977. "Koreans in America: An Emerging Ethnic Minority." *Amerasia Journal* vol. 4: 117-131.

———. 1982. "Occupation and Work Patterns of Korean Immigrants in Los Angeles." Pp. 49-73 in *Koreans in Los Angeles; Prospects and Promises*, edited by Eui- Young Yu, Earl H. Phillips, and Eun-Sik Yang. Koryo Research Institute, Los Angeles, CA.

Yun, Yo-Jun. 1977. "Early History of Korean Immigration to America." Pp.33-46 in *The Korean Diaspora: Historical and Sociological Studies of Korean Immigration and Assimilation in North America*, edited by Hyung-Chan Kim Santa Barbara: ABC-Clio, Inc.

Zimmer, Catherine and Howard Aldrich. 1987. "Resource Mobilization Through Ethnic Networks: Kinship and Friendship Ties of Shopkeepers in England." *Sociological Perspectives* vol. 30, no. 4 (October): 422-445.

Index